YOUR GUIDE TO
MASTERING THE CRAFT

WICCA
A Modern
Practitioner's Guide

Arin Murphy-Hiscock
Author of *The Green Witch*

Adams Media
New York London Toronto Sydney New Delhi

Adams Media
An Imprint of Simon & Schuster, Inc.
57 Littlefield Street
Avon, Massachusetts 02322

First Adams Media hardcover edition August 2019

ADAMS MEDIA and colophon are trademarks of Simon & Schuster.

For information about special discounts for bulk purchases, please contact Simon & Schuster Special Sales at 1-866-506-1949 or business@simonandschuster.com.

The Simon & Schuster Speakers Bureau can bring authors to your live event. For more information or to book an event contact the Simon & Schuster Speakers Bureau at 1-866-248-3049 or visit our website at www.simonspeakers.com.

Interior design by Michelle Kelly

Manufactured in the United States of America

10 9 8 7 6 5 4 3 2 1

Library of Congress Cataloging-in-Publication Data
Names: Murphy-Hiscock, Arin, author.
Title: Wicca: a modern practitioner's guide / Arin Murphy-Hiscock, author of The green witch.
Description: Avon, Massachusetts: Adams Media, 2019.
Includes bibliographical references and index.
Identifiers: LCCN 2019006900 | ISBN 9781507210741 (hc) | ISBN 9781507210758 (ebook)
Subjects: LCSH: Witchcraft.
Classification: LCC BF1566 .M795 2019 | DDC 133.4/3--dc23
LC record available at https://lccn.loc.gov/2019006900

ISBN 978-1-5072-1074-1
ISBN 978-1-5072-1075-8 (ebook)

Contains material adapted from the following title published by Adams Media, an Imprint of Simon & Schuster, Inc.: Solitary Wicca for Life by Arin Murphy-Hiscock, copyright © 2005, ISBN 978-1-59337-353-5.

Contents

Introduction

Wicca is a beautiful spiritual path that celebrates life, nature, and balance. As a beginner on this path, you learn something new every day and experience new sensations and feelings as you explore your spirituality. Now, as a more experienced practitioner, it is time to advance your skills and bring your learning to the next level.

As an intermediate Wiccan, you have reached a point where you want to know *more*, to really understand the *how and why* behind each basic step. You are now ready to begin crafting your own rituals step by step so that they reflect your personal interpretation of the Wiccan practice.

Wicca: A Modern Practitioner's Guide takes a fresh approach to this intermediate Wiccan learning. Inside these pages you'll take an in-depth look at the various elements of Wiccan practice and ritual, learn how to vary your practice, and challenge your existing notions of what Wicca is and what constitutes Wiccan tradition. You'll also explore simple and complex rites and reveal the inner workings of rituals to enhance celebration for every practitioner, whether you work alone or in a group environment.

True spiritual growth comes from challenge and change, so use the techniques and advice in this helpful guide to revisit the how and why of your path and expand your awareness of how your personal practice is put together. This book will help you reexamine the basics of Wicca from a more experienced position and learn how to create rich, rewarding rituals that will foster your personal growth in positive and joyous ways.

> You will notice that unless a ritual is specifically directed toward a unique god, the invoked God and Goddess are usually addressed as "Lord" and "Lady" to maintain a broad application. You are free to substitute the god-names you prefer to work with to personalize your invocations.

Chapter One

Practicing Wicca

This chapter will review the defining tenets of Wicca and differentiate traditional Wicca from the more flexible path of eclectic Wicca—the path upon which you most likely find yourself. Wicca is a flexible religion, not a free-form spiritual path. It has defined practices, beliefs, and ethical codes. Within this context, however, there exists great room for personal expression. For those who have practiced for several years, this chapter will serve to refresh and refine your understanding of what your spiritual path is.

The Origins of Wicca

It is inaccurate to say that Wicca is an ancient religion. The components and source material that combined to provide a base for Wicca may be of various vintages, but that doesn't make the finished product old by association. Wicca can be compared to a mosaic made from chips of stone gathered from a ruined temple or historical site. The material is ancient and imbued with history, but the mosaic created with it is an original piece of work. There is nothing shameful about a modern religion, particularly a modern religion that embraces love and life, and honors the past.

The roots of Wicca, as originally defined by British, Italian, and Northern Europe pre-Christian practices, probably honored a moon goddess and a hunter/vegetation god. These roots centered on fertility, and specific practices, such as celebrating festivals and holy days, were based on traditional localized agricultural celebrations.

The word *Wicca* has a variety of potential etymological sources, with roots in Old English and German as well as other Indo-European languages. The Indo-European root word *win* or *wik* has been incorporated into several European languages to describe such things as magic and religion, sorcery and holiness, and bending and shaping. The Indo-European root *wit* or *wid* is sometimes pulled into the equation as well: for example, the Old English word *witan* means "to know," and the element of wisdom is an important component of most religions as well as the practice of witchcraft. The Old German word *woken* means "to practice witchcraft," and the word *weihan* of the same language means "to consecrate," while the Old English word *wican* means "to bend." All these concepts reflect important aspects of the practice of modern Wicca. The actual word *wicca* is a variation of *wica*, an Old English word meaning a male practitioner of witchcraft (the female version is *wicce*, later associated specifically with a female diviner).

Gardnerian Wicca

Gardnerian Wicca (created by Gerald Gardner) is perhaps the best-known form of Wicca because of the publicity it generated in the mid-1950s. While Gardner claimed that it had been handed down whole, his new practice of Wicca actually included fragments of folk tradition, native British lore, Masonic and Rosicrucian elements, and practices taken from the Hermetic Order of the Golden Dawn (a nineteenth-century occult order).

Why Gerald Gardner chose to employ the word *Wicca* to describe the modern spiritual path is unknown, although the associated roots of the word all apply neatly to the tenets and ideologies of modern Wicca as it has developed over the past six decades.

Gardner created a precedent by using bits of belief and ritual from other religions and occult practices to create the structure and substance of Wicca. Over the past six decades the Wicca most people know has grown and expanded beyond Gardner's original vision. However, many people who call themselves Wiccan honestly believe that anything they do will qualify as Wicca because it's a form of personal spiritual expression—particularly if the new element of practice can be identified as a neo-Pagan approach—and the practice is taken from an ancient culture. This belief is false. While there is great freedom to move within the definition of Wicca, there are specific tenets that define the religion, and if those tenets are not adhered to, then it isn't Wicca, but rather an eclectic Pagan practice. (We'll discuss the basic Wiccan tenets later in this chapter.)

Wiccan versus Neo-Pagan

Wicca has influenced the neo-Pagan movement to such a degree that they have become almost synonymous—an erroneous connection. Many people mistakenly assume that they are Wiccan when they are in fact neo-Pagan. Many neo-Pagans react negatively to identifying with the term *Wicca* out of frustration at the perpetual misunderstanding.

Much of modern Wicca is derived from Celtic lore and practice, but other cultures have had significant influence as well. Other major influences on modern Wicca include the West Country practice, also from Britain; the Northern practice, from the Germanic and Scandinavian areas; and the Italian tradition of witchcraft, sometimes referred to as *Stregheria* or *La Vecchia Religione* (the old religion).

What is neo-Paganism? Author Isaac Bonewits defines it as:

[A] general term for a variety of movements [that attempt to] re-create, revive, or continue what their founders believed to

be the best aspects of the Paleopagan ways of their ancestors (or presumed predecessors). These were blended with modern humanistic, pluralistic, and inclusionary ideals, while attempting to eliminate inappropriate concepts, attitudes, and practices from the monotheistic, dualistic, or nontheistic worldviews. (Bonewits, *Witchcraft: A Concise Guide,* p. 142)

While Wicca is a neo-Pagan path, it is certainly not the only neo-Pagan path. Asatru, Heathenry, Druidry, and others also qualify as neo-Pagan. Wicca is simply one form of neo-Pagan expression.

Exploring Traditional Wicca

Traditional Wicca is a particular version of Wicca that has been practiced the same way for a long period of time. On a traditional path a group has an accepted and established structure and set of lore that remain constant and never change.

Typically, a traditional Wiccan must work in a group with others of the same tradition to learn from them and receive initiation to their secrets and private practices. It is theoretically impossible to practice Gardnerian or Alexandrian Wicca alone, as both of these traditional paths are initiatory. Gardnerian material is available in books and online, but simply using this material does not make one a Gardnerian nor a traditional Wiccan. Initiation must take place for those terms to apply to a Wiccan.

The Emergence of Eclectic Wicca

The past three decades saw such a rise of interest in Wicca that a new form of the religion, known as eclectic Wicca, emerged.

Eclectic Wicca has many traits in common with traditional Wicca, but it has a wider reach and is more adaptable and more permissive than the traditional forms of the religion. That being said, eclectic Wiccans can't stretch the religion out of shape to include any spiritual practice; eclectic Wiccan practice must still rest on the basic Wiccan tenets (which you'll be introduced to in a moment). Eclectic Wicca serves many practitioners around the world. It might very well be the most popular neo-Pagan path today. It is not in any way *inferior* to traditional Wicca—it is simply *different*.

> Understanding the underlying themes of your spiritual practice has a significant impact upon your psyche and spirit. It is important to remember that it is the spiritual message that counts, not just the ceremony itself. Piercing through the trappings to what the ritual *signifies* is the ultimate key. This means that you must match your chosen eclectic elements with great care, and test them out one by one within the confirmed context of your practice. Otherwise, the underlying effects can cancel each other out, or have a destructive effect upon your practice.

As long as your practice remains focused on the basic Wiccan tenets at all times, you can choose your own path in eclectic Wicca. Egyptian Wicca, for example, qualifies as eclectic Wicca, as it takes the traditional British-based Wicca as a template and plugs in the Egyptian deities, Egyptian myths and symbolism, and Egyptian-style holidays to supplement or enhance the eight Wiccan sabbats. Mixing Egyptian deities with Hellenic deities in the same practice, however, creates a different kind of eclectic Wicca. Incorporating a Buddhist meditation practice and a Slavic invocation makes it even more eclectic.

As in any religion, you cannot choose to follow only certain aspects of Wicca and still call yourself a Wiccan. You can, however, express your personal interpretation of that religion by adjusting your *method of practice*. For instance, you may choose to practice alone or in a group (or a mix of the two). As eclectic Wicca is a free-form religion that has no compulsory community activity, practicing alone is not frowned upon. There are several reasons why a Wiccan might choose to practice alone. Perhaps you prefer solitude to social environments, or there may not be other Wiccan practitioners in your area. Your spiritual practice may remain a personal and private thing by choice or by necessity. Whatever the reason, eclectic Wicca is extremely flexible and adapts very well to the needs of the solo practitioner, should that be your situation.

Be Cautious about Enacting Changes in Your Practice

Remember, though, that change for the sake of change is not necessarily good. Any spiritual technique must be practiced for some time before you see or feel the benefits, so beware of incorporating impressive-sounding aspects and then eliminating them before your spirit has had a chance to settle into them.

Constantly altering what you do to spiritually connect with the Divine serves only to confuse your subconscious. Because of the plateau effect, this is an easy trap for an intermediate Wiccan to fall into. When your development and noticeable progress level off, you can become frustrated because you can no longer feel drastic change occurring in your life. It can be extremely tempting to deem what you've been doing "no longer effective," toss it out, and cobble together a new structure. If you do this you will feel excited and challenged once again, but you will be reforming the basics—not building upon a solid foundation. Some intermediate Wiccans do this over and over, not realizing that they're creating their own obstacle by destroying everything they've established. A lack of *noticeable* growth does not indicate complacency; it often indicates boredom. And change in reaction to boredom can be dangerous. Change in response to thoughtful challenge is controlled and constructive, so if you decide to enact change, be certain that you have put much thought into why you are doing it.

What Are the Wiccan Tenets?

While Wicca shares some of its beliefs with other religions, philosophies, and spiritual paths, the combination provides a very unique religious practice. You know of the background of Wicca, but to define what you practice as Wicca you must adhere to specific tenets, regardless of whether you are eclectic or traditional. The practice of Wicca is generally defined by the following tenets.

A Belief in a Divine Source That Demonstrates Both Male and Female Energy

This belief is commonly stated as a belief in the God and Goddess. Sometimes this tenet is explained as the Divine being a spiritual force composed of both masculine and feminine energy, which in turn manifest in cultural perceptions as various gods and goddesses. Some Wiccans believe that instead of one divine source or entity, there are two very distinct deities—the Goddess and God—and they in turn manifest as the gender-related god-forms.

What is the truth about the gods of Wicca? Wicca is an experiential religion, meaning that you must undergo the experiences yourself in order to learn the mysteries of the religion. As a Wiccan, you must think and work through this mystery and come up with a conclusion of your own. Ask yourself some probing questions:

- Are all the gods one, and does that one simply choose different forms in which to manifest?
- Are the gods separate entities?
- What is my experience with the gods through ritual, and what can I glean from that experience?

A popular metaphor describes divine energy as a gemstone, and every facet on that gemstone as a different manifestation. These manifestations present themselves differently, but they are all, in the end, from the same divine energy source. In truth the manifestations are not the same—or there would be no need for different cultures to interpret the divine energy in different forms. Kali of the Hindu pantheon and the Morrighan of the pan-Celtic pantheon are both dark goddesses of destruction and war, but they are certainly not the same goddess, nor are their extended areas of association the same.

No gemstone found in nature is already faceted. A gemstone requires work by human hands to achieve those facets. Does divinity choose to present itself in these various differing forms, or is it human perception that distinguishes between them? Different cultures imagine gods and goddesses in very different ways. Over time those perceptions become more invested with energy and worship, further solidifying the form and perception of each deity.

Perhaps it is most accurate to say that humanity creates the gods out of the raw stuff of the Divine. We cannot know for certain. We can, however, construct a personal relationship with the gods, no matter what their origin, and learn more about ourselves through communing with them.

Some Wiccans describe themselves as *dualists*. A dualist believes in only two gods. In a Wiccan context this would be the God and Goddess. There is no room in dualism for any other deities. However, dualism denies the validity of the many different god-forms with whom many Wiccans communicate, and through whom many of us connect with the Divine.

A term often used in connection with Wicca is *polytheism*, which describes the belief in many separate gods. A polytheist is someone who truly and deeply believes in each god equally and distinctly (for example, that Kali has no relation to the Morrighan; that Isis and Nephthys are individual deities with no connection whatsoever; that Zeus and Jupiter are independent gods). The polytheist believes that every deity is an entity in and of itself, with no connection to anything larger or deeper. In some ways polytheism does not accurately reflect the complexity of the gods of Wicca.

A third term, and one that deserves serious consideration among Wiccans, is *henotheism*. This is the belief in one god without denying the existence of others. Henotheism recognizes that the deities with whom Wiccans work are valid without discounting any other god-forms. It is inclusive, rather than exclusive.

Which definition is correct? It depends on the practitioner. Each definition has pros as well as cons. As a Wiccan, you must carefully consider these definitions and decide which one best describes your beliefs and how you perceive deity.

Adherence to an Ethical Code As Outlined in the Wiccan Rede

The Wiccan Rede, sometimes referred to as the Witches' Rede, is a religion-specific version of an ethical guideline. The word *rede* comes from the Old English word *raedan*, meaning "to counsel or advise." This is precisely what the Wiccan Rede sets out to do: in its easily memorable rhyming format, the Rede guides Wiccans through a series of statements, warnings, and folk practices. The Rede is not a set of commandments. Punishment is not laid out for the Wiccan who does not follow the Rede. Instead, certain warnings encode the consequences of harmful action if chosen by the individual.

The origins of the Rede are contested, as is so much Wiccan material. The first published full form of the Rede is attributed to Lady Gwen Thompson, and it appeared in *Green Egg* magazine in 1975. Thompson claimed that the Rede had been handed down to her by her grandmother. Doreen Valiente wrote a different version, entitled "The Witches' Creed," which was released in her book *Witchcraft for Tomorrow* in 1978. Valiente's version may have been in use before that time and may have been based on earlier sources. Valiente's version addresses some of the same issues as Thompson's, but Thompson's version has proven to be more popular with its rhyming couplets.

The two extracts most commonly quoted from the Rede outline the very basis of the Wiccan ethical code. The first is the deceptively simple:

> *Eight words the Witches' Rede fulfill:*
> *If it harms none, do what thou will.*

This couplet is often shortened to the phrase, "An it harm none, do what you will." John Coughlin of the Wiccan Rede Project points out that Gardner makes direct reference to this Wiccan rule in his book *The Meaning of Witchcraft*. (In this book, as in his others, Gardner maintains that Wicca was handed to him fully formed by his teachers.)

> *[Wiccans] are inclined to the morality of the legendary Good King Pausol [sic], "Do what you like so long as you harm no one." But they believe a certain law to be important, "You must not use magic for anything which will cause harm to anyone, and if, to prevent a greater wrong being done, you must discommode someone, you must do it only in a way which will abate the harm." This involves every magical action being discussed first, to see that it can do no damage, and this induces a habit of mind to consider well the results of one's actions, especially upon others. This, you may say, is elementary Christianity. Of course it is; it is also elementary Buddhism, Hinduism, Confucianism, and Judaism, to name only a few.* (Gardner, p. 127)

Taken literally, the code dictates that you may not take any action if it causes harm. Many Wiccans struggle with where to draw the line in this belief. Every step you take can kill ants on a sidewalk—it is impossible not to harm any living thing by your actions. This is the ethical challenge of practicing Wicca. It is your responsibility to carefully consider both the magical and nonmagical consequences of your actions, make your decisions accordingly, and accept those consequences.

The often-quoted couplet is not an absolute law. Rather, it reminds us to think carefully about our actions and how they affect the environment around us. It also reminds the Wiccan that there is a constant flow of energy throughout the universe. Also key to this law is respect for the self, a belief inherent in the practice of Wicca. Undertaking action that harms the self is as wrong as undertaking action that harms another.

Gardner isn't the only one to have hit upon this saying. In controversial Thelemic magician Aleister Crowley's *The Book of the Law*, a book said to be channeled from an angelic entity named Aiwass in 1904, he writes: "Who calls us Thelemites will do no wrong, if he look but close into the word. For there are therein Three Grades, the Hermit, and the Lover, and the man of Earth. Do what thou wilt shall be the whole of the Law." (Crowley, 1:40)

Intermediate Wiccans often get hung up on the issue of will. One of the most challenging things about taking action is figuring out what your true will is. The Rede implies that action without careful forethought and examination of desire and motive can be harmful. Only by knowing and understanding our true will can we harness and focus willpower effectively and efficiently.

The moral and ethical guidelines set out in the Rede are further developed by the second most often quoted couplet, concerning the Three-Fold Law:

Ever mind the rule of three: what you send out comes back to thee.

This is sometimes reworded to read:

Mind the Three-Fold Law you should, three times bad and three times good.

This couplet outlines the belief that the energy attached to any good or bad action that a Wiccan performs will be revisited upon the practitioner three-fold (also known as the Law of Return). The three-fold attribution is specific to the practice of Wicca, but the general law of cosmic consequence to an action or behavior is not unique. The Buddhist concept of karma is similar to the Law of Return. The Ontario Consultants on Religious Tolerance call the widely held belief that an individual should treat others in a positive fashion "the ethics of reciprocity."

Almost every religion has a version of "the Golden Rule," an expression found in philosophical or sacred texts that encourages the individual to behave in a positive and thoughtful fashion.

The Wiccan Rede urges followers of the Wiccan path to perform positive actions and avoid deliberately harmful actions. Intermediate practitioners often run into the issue of what constitutes a rightful action and what constitutes wrongful action. Situations can be cloudy, with no clearly defined right and wrong choices; sometimes there are only choices that are less bad than others. This can lead to frustration, but do not despair: the struggle is a sign of your developing awareness. Continue to question your choices and actions, for as you do you will know that you are making no prejudgment and that you are taking each circumstance and evaluating it as a new experience. This is as it should be.

The Wiccan Mythos

The Wiccan mythos constitutes a series of allegories and stories that describe the lives of the Goddess and God. Some of the most popular and well-known stories include:

- The descent of the Goddess into the underworld to learn the mystery of death
- The birth of the Sun God at Midwinter
- The celebration of the union of the Goddess and God at Beltaine
- The battle of the Oak King and the Holly King at the summer and winter solstices
- The sacrifice of the God at the harvest

Part of the Wiccan mythos also involves the belief that we all contain a spark of divine energy within us. Remember: We are *of* the gods, but we are not ourselves gods. We reflect the Divine, but we are not Divinity itself. In Wicca we are proof of the power of the gods. We may channel the gods, commune with them, and manifest their attributes in our lives, but we are not their equals, as writer Dilys Dana Pierson states so clearly:

I am frustrated and, yes, sometimes angry. Popular authors tell me that "I am the Goddess." No, I am not. She is immortal; She is everlasting; She is the source from whom I seek solace and inspiration and guidance. All too familiar with my faults and weaknesses, I am aware that I, unlike the Goddess, am mortal. I seek the Divine, I pray to the Divine, I aspire to the Divine, and while...I recognize that of the Divine in every being, I am not the Divine. I am of her, but I am not her.

The spiritual path we choose to follow and celebrate is an expression of that spark of divinity within us. We are a part of gods, as they are a part of us, but we will never be able to wholly encompass the magnitude of what they are.

This leads to the idea of service. Some Wiccans say that they "serve the gods," which can be a misleading statement for newer Wiccans to hear, because we do not necessarily consider ourselves subservient to gods. We devote ourselves joyfully to working *with* the gods, in an attempt to make the world a better place for humanity, the animal kingdom, the world of plants, and all creatures known and unknown. We do the work of the gods in the way that we can for harmony and balance.

This is what the Wiccan mythos essentially teaches us: Everything is change, everything moves in cycles, and in this change there is balance. To achieve harmony, this ever-changing balance must occur. As members of this world, we have the honor and responsibility to work within the world toward this balance.

Tolerance for Other Spiritual Paths and Religions

The phrase "There is no one true way" is often heard in Wiccan communities, and it is a direct reflection of the Wiccan approach to the Divine. Wiccans respect all spiritual paths and religions as equally valid methods of uniting with the Divine. Truth is attainable through different methods. Wiccans firmly believe in the freedom to practice religion according to an individual's own preferences, as long as those practices do not infringe upon the rights and freedoms of others.

Belief in Reincarnation/Afterlife

As cycles are honored in nature, they are honored in our lives. The basic life cycle of birth, life, death is honored, but the cycle does not end there. The belief that the cycle commences once again is an integral part of how a Wiccan sees the world.

Wiccans believe that our soul, spirit, or personal energy will travel onward in the cycle of life and be reborn in another individual. This cycle continues until the soul has learned all the lessons it has set out to learn, and the soul then leaves the cycle to retire to a place of joy and regeneration (sometimes referred to as the Summerland). While beliefs such as this are commonly held within Wicca, there is no singular and clearly defined afterlife concept for Wiccans. You may have thought upon this subject and developed your own theories. If not, the place of death within the cycle of life is certainly a worthy subject to meditate upon.

Respect for Nature

While Wiccans honor the principle of divinity within all things, we do not worship trees, hills, or stones. The word *pantheism* is sometimes used to describe neo-Pagan paths. This term is often misunderstood as meaning the worship of nature, but it actually means to recognize the Divine in all places, or to identify the Divine with the universe. The root word *pan* means "everywhere," and Wiccans certainly believe that their gods are accessible in all places, at all times.

Wiccans believe that divinity is immanent in nature and honor it accordingly in different ways. Many of us celebrate the Wheel of the Year as it manifests in seasonal festivals, most commonly through the eight sabbats. Not all Wiccan traditions celebrate all eight sabbats, however, and not all Wicca-like paths celebrate the same eight festivals around the same time.

The term *animism* refers to the belief that every inanimate thing possesses a spirit. In this definition an animistic religion includes a belief that trees, rocks, streams, and hills all have awareness. To an extent Wiccans do believe this and often refer to it as the *genius loci*, the "spirit of place." This belief is usually the result of developing an ability to sense the energy associated with a place or natural object.

The main core of Wiccan practice and belief is based on the concept of fertility—the interaction between the natural male and female principles to produce new life and advance the natural cycle. One of the ways a Wiccan attunes to nature is by harmonizing their personal energy with the seasonal cycle. Most commonly this is achieved by regular ritual to honor the seasons and communication with the earth at its various stages of the seasonal cycle. Harmony is also achieved by living an environmentally responsible life.

The Deliberate Decentralization of Wicca

Eclectic Wicca is so fluid (apart from the basic Wiccan precepts) that it is difficult to find two Wiccans who agree completely about every aspect of their religion, even the definition or application of the basic tenets previously outlined. The design of Wicca encourages decentralization. There can never be a governing body that makes decisions affecting all Wiccans, everywhere, around the world.

The deliberate decentralization of Wicca has its benefits and its drawbacks. Each Wicca book you read will present a point of view contradictory in some way to the previous book you read, and this can challenge how you perceive and practice Wicca. You can get bogged down in pondering how to practice without getting something "wrong." Remember always that no one can tell you what to do, other than to adhere to the basic tenets that define Wicca—this is one of the safeguards built into our religion. Any author you read, or any Wiccan you speak with online or in person, may have their own confirmed ways of practicing the religion beyond those tenets, but that person has no right to force them upon you.

Being responsible for your own path also means that you carry a heavy burden: you must make the difficult decisions, and you must think through every moral and ethical challenge for yourself. This can be tiring, but it enables you to develop as a spiritual person. Tolerance and open-mindedness are key to learning and growing, both as a Wiccan and as a spiritual person in general.

The Thirteen Principles of Wiccan Belief

In April 1974 seventy-three witches came together in Minneapolis to form the temporary American Council of Witches. This council made the first attempt ever to outline and record a common set of beliefs held by Wiccans in the United States. It was an enormous undertaking. The results did nothing to limit Wiccans; instead, the council helped define the Wiccan path. Reading this document can help you clarify what you believe as a Wiccan, and rereading it at regular intervals can help remind you of why you have chosen to walk this path.

Note that in the document (and this is very common elsewhere) these Wiccans call themselves witches. By this point in your study of Wicca you understand that the terms *Wiccan* and *witch* are not always synonymous; the latter indicates a magical practice with or without a personal connection to nature, and the former indicates a specific, defined religion and spiritual path.

The Pros and Cons of Solitary and Coven-Based Wicca

There are both pros and cons to practicing as a solitary Wiccan or as a member of a Wiccan coven.

Many older books in metaphysical shops and documents on the Internet insist that Wicca must be performed in a group environment, as part of a magical partnership with one other person of the opposite sex, or only after initiation by a more experienced Wiccan. Requirements such as these tend to be associated with traditional Wicca, which relies on an established and constant structure. For those Wiccans who prefer to practice in a group, these types of traditional requirements can be not only acceptable but also desirable.

For Wiccans who practice a form of eclectic Wicca, the emphasis on maintaining cohesion and practicing in an established fashion is less important. A solitary Wiccan may not have access to other more experienced practitioners, but they can still acquire new learning by trying things out, by taking associated courses or workshops pertinent to spirituality and spiritual practice, or by reading more advanced or specialized books. There is no eclectic requirement (nor is there a tenet) stating that Wiccan practice must happen within a group, a partnership, or any other kind of social or community context. That said, covens do not exist only in the practice of traditional Wicca; often like-minded eclectic Wiccans assemble to practice together.

The Pros and Cons of Working with a Coven

You may be curious about the benefits of working in a coven environment. Ideally, a coven provides a family atmosphere and supports and encourages its members. A coven collects resources as a unit and shares responsibility for organizing, planning, writing, and leading rituals, and hosting meetings. An established coven has a strong, inspirational level of commitment. Members can learn from each other and seek guidance from the more experienced practitioners in the group. If the coven is well integrated, there can be the benefit of well-focused and amplified energy raised when magic is performed. A coven develops a unique group-mind made up of all the individuals within it. In a coven there is always the opportunity for discourse and discussion, and the opportunity for sharing; different minds and different points of view offer continual mental and spiritual stimulation. A coven also provides an established community to perform rites of passage for its members or the families of members. The coven can confirm or validate experiences that an individual member may be having, shedding light on the process of development and learning, and providing support for the challenges each member faces in their ongoing spiritual quest. There will be a variety of skills found within a coven, as each individual is interested in various topics and experienced in different areas.

There are certain difficulties that a coven must work to overcome. Trust in other coven members is essential, as confidentiality is an important aspect of coven work. While there is the opportunity to share personal experiences or problems, if the coven is not solid and if perfect trust does not exist between all the members, the issue of confidentiality and trust can be an uncomfortable one. A coven offers the opportunity for deep intimacy of a spiritual nature, which can be ambiguous if that perfect trust is absent. The discretion of each and every member must be sure for a coven to function smoothly and to the benefit of all.

Also keep in mind that not all covens are Wiccan. The word *witch* is sometimes used as a synonym for a Wiccan, but it is a word that makes many Wiccans uncomfortable. A witch practices magic, as a Wiccan sometimes does, and a witch can choose to honor deity in whatever form they choose; but a witch is not bound by the Wiccan Rede or other Wiccan tenets. A substantial portion of Wiccan practice echoes (and is likely based upon) the traditions of those named as witches in previous centuries, but Wicca itself is not synonymous with witchcraft. Some non-Wiccan covens assemble simply to perform magic. A Wiccan coven may perform magic together, but the primary focus is on honoring the gods and promoting self-improvement through meditation and communication with those deities.

The more members there are in the group, the more challenging coordination and time management become. Unfortunately, the chances of personal conflict also increase with the number of people who become involved, as does the potential for power struggles between those who wish to hold more responsibility or prestige.

A coven that practices the same way all the time can run the risk of becoming mired in dogma. As with any group of people, rules must be set down and compromises must be made for smooth social interaction to occur. Finally, the high level of commitment necessary may stress the members.

The Pros and Cons of Working As a Solitary Eclectic Wiccan

A solo practitioner has every opportunity to obtain as rewarding and as spiritual a practice as a Wiccan who works within a coven. A solitary Wiccan will have a different experience, but two Wiccans within the same coven will also have different experiences. Every single individual interacts with the energies of the world in a different way, and everyone ends up with a different perception of the experience. Naturally, all of us will internalize and assimilate the lessons of our lives via a different method, and reach a personal conclusion unique to ourselves. We learn what we need to learn.

A solo practitioner possesses the individual freedom to do whatever they want within the tenets of the Wiccan structure. As a solitary Wiccan, you have the freedom of choice and the final say in how and when to practice; there is no one else to interfere (except the gods, but we will discuss communication with deities later). The focus is always on personal growth as opposed to the growth of the group. Apart from the Wiccan Rede and the ethical responsibilities outlined in the tenets, the only ethics you have to consider are your own. No oath or promise of confidentiality is required, as the only oaths and secrets you can give away are your own. Scheduling becomes easier, as there is only one person to consider. Working alone also improves your sense of responsibility and self-reliance, and teaches you to trust yourself.

Some of these positive aspects can also be challenges. Self-governing can be a heavy responsibility at times. Working solo may lead to a sense of loneliness and disconnection from the world around you. The lack of structure and stimulation provided by other minds can sometimes lead to an apathetic practice, or a lapsed Wiccan. Practicing alone can be costly if you don't watch your budget or approach things creatively. Certain aspects of your practice may leave you uncertain as to their pertinence or meaning. Without others to provide feedback, you can experience difficulty in evaluating your own progress. Sometimes, too, you may feel adrift because there is no established community through which rites of passage may be performed, or initiation into another level given.

All of these challenges can be turned to your benefit, however. Throughout this book you will encounter rituals and discussion to make you think about your practice, and evaluate how you see your spirituality and apply it to your everyday life.

At its heart Wicca is founded on what are referred to as the *mysteries*. Essentially, mysteries are deep, soul-changing realizations and lessons obtained via encounters with the Divine in some way, shape, or form. Mysteries cannot be taught by writing them down and passing them to someone else to read. It is possible to write down the actual words—for instance, *All gods are one god*, which is an aspect of one of the mysteries. But reading these words on the page is very different from knowing them intellectually and understanding them on a deep emotional and spiritual level in a flash of soul-searing epiphany. The former, you know. The latter, you *know*. You don't learn a mystery; you *experience* it.

How does a solitary Wiccan experience the mysteries? The same way any Wiccan encounters them: in life lessons, through ritual, and through practice and the acquisition of personal experience. A coven Wiccan may have coven elders to help them through the process of understanding the mystery, and the coven may provide a ready-made context for the experiences, but the experience is in no way superior to that of a solitary practitioner. In fact, you may benefit more from working through the mysteries on your own, as you must do all the work of relating the experience to your life and personal belief system.

Chapter Two

Sacred Space

This chapter presents various techniques for creating sacred space, and suggests appropriate times to use sacred space instead of a circle.

What Are Sacred Spaces?

In a Wiccan ritual the bulk of what you do is handle, raise, weave, and channel energy. All these tasks require large amounts of concentration, and therefore it makes sense to perform them in an area that is secure from distraction or interference.

There are two very different ways you can create a safe space in which to work. The first and most common method is to create a circle—a sphere-shaped energy barrier around you and your workspace. The second method, which is often overlooked, is to simply create sacred space. This may puzzle you for a moment, particularly since some of the authors you've read probably use both terms to describe the same thing. Intermediate students are astounded when I tell them that a circle isn't always necessary for the type of work they might be planning.

When you began practicing Wicca you probably obsessed over raising or casting a circle before every ritual or spell, and wondered if you were doing it right. Practicing and perfecting the circle is important for beginning Wiccans. After you've become adept at a circle, however, you sometimes don't need to use one anymore—sacred space may be all you require, depending on the working you're planning. Many of the simpler and less dramatic Wiccan rituals can be performed in sacred space without casting a formal circle.

Sacred space offers you an area cleansed of distractions and lingering energy. The purified area is appropriate for meditation, simple offerings, and simple honoring rituals. It's often enough to create sacred space in an area you know well or practice in often. If you are lucky enough to have a temple or dedicated worship space in your home, then that is your permanent sacred space.

Why Should You Use Sacred Space?

The most basic reason to use sacred space instead of a circle is because the act of creating sacred space is less intense and less stressful on you.

Sacred space allows you to still interact with the world beyond it; it's less of a barrier than a circle is. When you use sacred space you make the existing environment holy as opposed to creating a whole new environment. You remain open to the good energies in the area and not sealed away from them.

Sacred space is a wonderful alternative to a circle if you seek to create a harmonious atmosphere for a family gathering, particularly if the attendees are of mixed spiritualities and if the space you are using is unfamiliar to you. It can be created without the knowledge of others, for it purifies and harmonizes the energy of the area, removing distracting, harmful, or stale energy and leaving a positive and smooth feeling in its place.

What makes sacred space different from a circle? A circle is a consciously constructed space that partially overlaps both our world and the world of the gods. The resulting area is "between the worlds," not wholly in one or the other. This space is sometimes referred to as a temple, because it combines aspects of our world and the plane of the Divine. Sacred space is a place of peace and calm, but it is not necessarily "between the worlds." Sacred space is what goes into the circle, or it can simply exist on its own.

Creating sacred space for other people who may not share your beliefs does not manipulate them in any way, nor does it disrespect their choice of religion. You are offering them a peaceful and balanced environment in which to study, discuss, eat, or mingle. Try creating sacred space before a dinner gathering during the week, when everyone is tired and stressed; everyone attending the dinner will be better able to relax in the more serene energy. Sacred space is a flexible and adaptable application with plenty of informal and nonritual uses. Remember that nonritual does not mean nonspiritual. For Wiccans, daily life is a spiritual experience.

Steps for Creating Sacred Spaces

There are four basic steps to creating sacred space. If you've been practicing for a while, you will likely look at these steps and realize that you do most of them, just all at once. Separating the steps in this rite will help you gain full understanding of what is happening, and this will give you a better grip on the foundations of your practice. This isn't a question of relearning the basics; it's a question of exploring the fullness and richness of your spiritual path. Again, we are seeking to reveal the *why* behind what you do.

- **Create internal sacred space.** This involves eliminating thoughts and energies of the outside world from your presence to create a calm and ritual-ready psyche.
- **Cleanse.** Physically clean and neaten the area you will be using for your ritual so that you have a tidy and clear space in which to work.

- **Purify.** This is the magical counterpart to cleansing. Purification removes negative energy.
- **Consecrate.** This step entails the blessing of the space in some fashion. Consecration is what most Wiccans think of when they think of creating sacred space.

From here you can go on to cast a circle if you so desire, or if your ritual requires it. Otherwise, working within the sacred space is perfectly acceptable.

Creating a Tranquil Internal Sacred Space

Before you engage in any workings, it is best to calm your spirit and your mind by creating a tranquil inner base from which you can work to create physical and spiritual sacred space. There are a variety of ways to do this, including meditation, centering and grounding, and generally balancing your energy.

Begin by clearing your mind, and take a few minutes to relax your body. Taking even five minutes to meditate will help you attain a frame of mind conducive to creating sacred space. If you like to use aromatherapy, now may be the time to release a scent such as lavender into the air, or to burn a favorite calming incense. Centering (see Chapter Four) is also an ideal way to begin the process of creating sacred space.

The ritual bath or shower and purification with a smudge stick or incense are other popular methods of creating internal sacred space. Suggestions for these techniques follow in the sections on cleansing and purifying.

Cleansing the Physical

Cleansing the self and the physical space for ritual removes the distraction that comes from dirt and clutter, both mental and physical. Physical clutter creates chaotic energy, as do dust and residue. Sweeping the floor with a regular broom and dustpan, cleaning off your altar or workspace, and tidying the general area will minimize distraction while you work.

This step includes cleansing yourself. Following are some quick but effective methods of cleansing your body prior to working ritual. While this step technically focuses on physical cleansing, the ingredients in this bath scrub also encourage you to mentally and emotionally prepare yourself for creating sacred space. If you do not wish to use the bath scrub, you can take a regular bath or shower to cleanse instead, focusing on the water as a cleansing element.

Cleansing Bath Scrub

This scrub can be used in a shower or bath before you move on to create sacred space (or cast your circle). Remember to use warm—not hot—water; it will be less stressful on your system. (Do not use this scrub on your face. If you have sensitive skin: blend the lemon zest, flowers, and oils and omit the salt; rub the mixture gently into your skin prior to your bath or shower and rinse off.)

What You Need:

- 2 teaspoons lavender flowers (fresh or dried)
- Lidded jar that will fit at least 2 cups scrub
- ½ cup sea salt
- 1 cup fine Epsom salt

- Small glass bowl
- ½ cup sweet almond or jojoba oil
- 3 drops lavender essential oil
- 3 drops frankincense essential oil
- 1 teaspoon lemon zest (fresh or dried)
- Damp washcloth

What to Do:

1. Purify the ingredients according to your preferred method. Grind the flowers finely while you empower them for cleansing and purification of body, mind, and spirit.
2. In the covered jar shake the two salts together. In the small bowl blend the oils together. Open the jar and add the oil blend to the salt. Close the jar and shake to blend thoroughly. Open the jar and sprinkle the lemon zest and flowers over the oil and salt blend. Close the jar and shake to blend one final time.
3. To use the salt scrub once you are in the bath or shower, place about 1 tablespoon in the center of a clean, damp washcloth or in the palm of your hand. Gently rub the salts against your skin, visualizing the loosening of any negative energy that is clinging to you. Feel the purifying salt, lavender, frankincense, and lemon soaking into your body, cleansing your aura and calming your mind.
4. When you feel cleansed, rinse the salt scrub and the negative energy away with the water of your bath or shower.
5. When you step out of the bath, dry yourself gently with a clean towel.

Once your body and mind have been cleansed, you can move on to cleansing your space. Put away loose papers, piles of books, clothes, toys, and other clutter in the area you intend to use for ritual. Once the physical clutter is cleared away, clean and polish the surfaces of the area with empowered household cleaning supplies, or with a magical wash, such as the following cleansing wash.

Cleansing Wash

This wash can be added to the water used for mopping or scrubbing floors, or to a spray bottle to mist over an area. Alternatively, spray it on a soft cloth to wipe down objects. The wash is also ideal for adding a touch of extra cleansing energy to your regular housework.

What You Need:

- Medium glass bowl
- 1 cup spring water (bottled or fresh)
- 1 tablespoon lemon juice
- 1 drop rose water
- 1 pinch salt
- Glass jar or bottle with lid, cap, or cork
- Label and pen

What to Do:

1. Purify your ingredients according to your preferred method. In the glass bowl blend the spring water, lemon juice, rose water, and salt, empowering them for cleansing. Decant the wash into the jar or bottle and cap it securely. Label as

"Cleansing Wash" with the date and the ingredients. Store in the refrigerator for up to one week.

2. If you intend to mop your ritual area, add nine drops of this wash to four cups of water. Otherwise, prepare a spray bottle as follows: Add nine drops to a cup of spring water in a spray bottle and shake to blend. If you intend to sweep with a regular household broom, spray the bristles of your broom before sweeping. Otherwise, lightly spray a soft cloth and wipe down the furniture, walls, and floor of your intended ritual area.

Purifying Spaces and Energies

Again, purifying the self and the area are both important. While cleansing deals with physical dirt, purification deals specifically with the negative energy that clutters up an area. It can be done by burning appropriate incense or by sweeping in a counterclockwise motion with a besom. Standing in the center of your space and visualizing a ball of white light materializing in the center, then growing outward to drive away negativity, will also purify the space, although many Wiccans prefer to purify in a more physical fashion.

Before you begin this step, do a quick energy reading of the space by extending your senses and walking through it, walking around it, or standing in the center and turning slowly. Evaluate the feeling of the energy around you. This entails lowering your personal shields, which can be tricky if you've never worked consciously with personal shields before. (If this is confusing or you're not sure how to sense energy, see Chapter Four.) Once you have an idea of what the energy in the area is like, you can better address what needs to be removed.

A popular method of purification is to use salt. Salt is a naturally purifying substance, and you can either sprinkle it sparingly in the area you wish to purify, or add a pinch to a cup of water and sprinkle drops of it from your fingers for easier application. Alternatively, you may choose to use a besom to sweep the energy of your area clear of negativity.

You may notice that the Cleansing Bath Scrub (see recipe earlier in this chapter) touches on purifying the mind and aura as well as the body. If you prefer, you can simply take a regular bath or shower to cleanse your body, and afterward use a smudging incense such as the following to purify your mind and spirit while you purify the energy of the ritual area.

Purifying Incense

Burning this incense on a charcoal tablet—available from religious or occult supply shops—is a traditional form of purifying energy that is found in various cultures.

What You Need:

- 1 tablespoon frankincense resin
- Mortar and pestle
- 1 tablespoon crumbled or powdered dried sage
- 1 teaspoon sandalwood powder
- 1 teaspoon cedar powder
- Charcoal tablet
- Matches or a lighter
- Heatproof dish or censer lined with sand or salt
- Feather or fan for wafting (optional)

What to Do:

1. Purify the ingredients according to your preferred method. Gently crush the resin into powder or fine grains with the mortar and pestle. Gently add the sage, sandalwood powder, and cedar powder to the resin and blend evenly.
2. Carefully light a charcoal tablet using matches or a lighter and place it on the sand or salt in the heatproof dish or censer. When the sparking has ceased and the charcoal glows red, it is ready (some prefer to wait until there is a fine layer of ash over the surface). While you wait, visualize your area slowly glowing brighter with a purifying white light.
3. Sprinkle no more than a teaspoon of the incense on the glowing charcoal tablet. As the smoke begins to billow and rise, waft it toward you with your hands and allow it to touch your body. Waft the smoke all around you and visualize it nullifying the negative energy that clings to you.
4. Place another teaspoon of the incense on the tablet when the smoke ceases, and waft it around your area. Some like to use a feather or a fan to aid the dispersal of the smoke. As you waft the smoke, visualize the negative energy of the area lifting and dissipating before the white light and the energy of the purifying smoke.

It is important to remember that purification is the spiritual or energy equivalent of the physical cleansing. In this step you are not blessing or sanctifying the space; you are removing negative energy. There are many methods by which this may be done, and one of my favorites is to use a crystal dedicated only to the use of absorbing negative energy. I use a chunk of very dark smoky quartz, about the size of my fist, which I have affectionately labeled the Black Hole for its desire to drink an area dry of doubtful, negative, actively harmful, or simply excess energy.

If you prefer to purify using a stone instead of incense, research the properties of the stones that draw you and find out which kinds would serve as absorbers or deflectors of negative energy. Smoky quartz just happens to be an excellent stone that possesses qualities of protection, transformation of negative energy, and balancing of energy.

As everyone interacts differently with stones and crystals, you may choose to experiment with such stones as obsidian or a clear quartz point in your purification. These stones tend to be projective, rather than receptive like smoky quartz. Rather than visualizing the negative energy being absorbed into the stone, imagine the stone repelling the energy away from your space.

Purifying with a Stone

Before you use your chosen stone to purify a space, cleanse it and program or charge it with the purpose of purification; not every stone is as single-minded as the Black Hole. Remember to cleanse your stone(s) often to get rid of any negative energy that may cling to it.

What You Need:

- Stone or crystal

What to Do:

1. Beginning at the perimeter of your area, slowly walk counterclockwise in smaller and smaller circles, spiraling in toward

the center. As you do this, hold out the crystal and visualize it sucking in all the doubtful and negative energy contained within the space. If there is a place that feels as if it has collected more negative energy, pause there and move the crystal around and up and down slowly, until you feel that the energy has been absorbed.

2. Finish in the center of the space. As an added precaution you can leave the crystal lying on the floor to allow it to draw in the last vestiges of doubtful energy.

Consecrating Your Sacred Spaces

Once both you and your ritual space have been physically cleansed and spiritually purified, the space is ready to be consecrated. To consecrate means to sanctify, and this is the definitive step that makes the space sacred.

For Wiccans this step often means presenting or sealing the space to the Divine. It is not enough to simply sanctify the space with words or gestures. The point of creating sacred space is to consecrate it to a specific sacred *purpose*. The purpose will, of course, depend on why you are creating the sacred space in the first place.

If you do not wish to consecrate the space in the name of a specific deity or deities, you can do what many other Wiccans do: sanctify the space by introducing the energy of each element. Some Wiccans light candles to honor the four physical elements, sometimes with a fifth to indicate Spirit or the source of all. Others use the physical elements to consecrate the space, asking for the blessings of each element as they move clockwise around the physical space with each element in a preferred sequence. This elemental blessing is commonly done with one or three pinches of salt in water, sprinkled around the perimeter of the space, followed by incense, which represents both fire by the glowing coal and air by the scent released.

Another method by which the space may be sanctified is by standing in the center of the area and channeling energy from both earth and sky. Center your own energy within your body, then ground to the energy of the earth in your usual way. (If you need a quick refresher on the grounding process, consult Chapter Four.) Once you are securely grounded, reach up from your energy center and connect with the energy of the sky. If it's easier to think of connecting to the sun, the moon, or the stars, then focus on doing that instead. Once you have connected to the sky energy, allow it to flow down your energy connection into your energy center. Draw up the earth energy from the ground, and allow it to mingle with the sky energy. Allow this dual energy to radiate outward from your center to fill the space.

You may think that channeling energy from both earth and sky sounds a bit like casting a circle, as it encompasses accessing energy and putting it into your space. When you cast a circle, you are consciously channeling energy and directing it according to your will, forming it into a defined barrier. When creating sacred space in this fashion, you are serving as a conduit through which natural energy flows, but you are not directing the energy. You simply allow it to flow through you and through the space, thereby shifting the resident energy from mundane to sanctified. In this instance you do not force the energy to form into something defined and solid, such as a circle—you allow it to flow, and then you release it. It is important to consciously release that flow of energy from both sky and earth to stop the process. Otherwise, you remain an open conduit, and the resulting energy flowing through your energy center can overcharge or unbalance you. If you are not used to "grounding up," you may wish to disengage that connection altogether and rely on the more commonly used earth grounding as you carry on.

After Your Ritual

Unlike a circle, which is a formal space between the worlds, sacred space does not need to be dismantled or desanctified. If you make sure to ground and otherwise clear away the energy you bring in while performing the actions that constitute the purpose for your sacred space, then there should remain nothing to dispel or take down. Sacred space is pure space; there is no need to dismantle purity. Because there is no dismissal procedure to perform as there is when you use a circle, your ritual may feel awkward and unfinished. To firmly signal that the ritual is over, get into the habit of using a formal statement, such as "This ritual is ended. I go in peace," to give your activity a sense of conclusion.

How long does sacred space last? It depends on the area in which you create it. If you create sacred space in a room of your home that does not see a lot of traffic, then the sanctity of the area will linger longer than the sacred space you might create at a public mall, for example. The length of time that the sacred space will last is directly connected to how much other energy flows through the space on a regular basis, and what kind of energy that might be.

Chapter Three

Casting Circles

This chapter explores intermediate techniques for casting circles, applications, and visualizations. You'll also learn how to work correctly within a circle and how to dismantle it safely.

The Meaning of the Circle

The circle is not temporary sacred space; it is a temporary temple—a formal place in which a Wiccan may work and worship in safety. Remember that:

- Wiccans consider the entire world, material and nonmaterial, to possess inherent sacred energy.
- Wiccans consider themselves to be containers of a spark of divine energy.

These two beliefs working together mean that we can formally designate any area as sacred at any time, as the Divine within us recognizes the holiness inherent in the physical location through the ceremony of raising a circle.

Circles were once used in occult practices as protection from evil waiting to attack. Wiccans today don't believe in an abstract concept of evil roaming the earth, looking for unwary individuals to ensnare. Therefore, a circle's primary purpose in modern Wicca is not to defend from evil but to separate us from everyday surroundings and place us within a holy zone closer to the gods. A circle's secondary purpose is to contain the energy you raise with defined intent. Although a circle acts as a magical container, holding the energy you're working with, when you release that energy with intention, the energy passes through your circle without breaking it. As part of its secondary purpose the circle concentrates the energy you raise within its limited space until you are ready to release the energy toward your intended goal. Finally, a circle's tertiary purpose is to define the boundary of your workspace. In a circle your actions are separated from the everyday world and you engage in a greater intensity of focus.

On a physical level you create a circle by walking around a perimeter of your intended workspace, often three times. Simply walking in a circle three times defines the circle's space in your mind, but it does not create the energy barrier Wiccans understand the circle to be. For the circle to exist both in the physical realm and in the mental and spiritual realms, you must also visualize the circle with clear intent, channeling energy into that visualization until it takes form. The energy used for channeling mainly comes from the earth, to which you ground yourself prior to raising the circle, but also partially from within the caster, as you must guide that energy with your will.

Beginner Wiccans understand the concept of walking the circle, but it takes a while before they channel energy with confidence as they raise one. Casting a circle begins as an act of faith, to an extent; you *believe* the circle is there. Over time a Wiccan realizes that the energy within the designated space is very different from the energy outside it. This concept is something you learn—for example, if you have to cut a door in your circle to fetch something you've forgotten and feel the difference between the energy within the circle and beyond it. More proof comes when you've done a strenuous and taxing ritual and dismantle the circle to be met with a cool breeze and relaxed energy—a direct contrast to the heat and higher vibrations you felt while the circle was still up.

There's nothing wrong with casting and dismantling circles just for practice. A circle is a step within a larger formal sequence, nothing more. Don't feel obliged to include the invocations and ritual workings that you normally do in a formal ritual. Instead of raising it with the intention for it to be a temple space, practice raising it with the intention of refining your circle-management skills. Before you experiment with the more advanced techniques of circle dissolution, make sure you ground and dismiss all the extra energy inside your circle.

The Vocabulary of Circles

Some Wiccans say that they "cast" the circle, which may be a reference to "casting" a spell. When you cast something, you toss it up and out. Perhaps, once upon a time, witches drew their protective circles by throwing something up into the air, which then spread out and settled to the ground. The term *casting* can be misleading in describing the creation of a circle, however, because it encourages us to think in a single dimension.

The term *raising* a circle has different mental associations. Raising a circle sounds like you're building it from a base and lifting it above you, which is exactly what you do when you create a circle. A circle isn't a flat ring, nor is it simply a dome over you. Your "circle" is actually a sphere covering you both above and below your workspace, as if you were standing in a bubble. We draw a circle, but we envision a sphere growing out of the line we draw; it's a circle in three dimensions, a shell that allows the sacred space within the circle to exist between the worlds.

Removing or unmaking a circle can also be described several ways: dismantling, unspinning, dissolving, taking it down, or lowering. Again, each of these descriptions carries different allusions to how the technique may have received its name.

To further confuse you, some traditions and authors refer to *creating* the circle as opening the circle (as in opening it for use), while other traditions refer to *dismantling* the circle as opening it (as in opening it to release the energy tied up in it).

You can use whatever word you like, as long as it meshes with your visualizations and helps you think of your circle as a complete sphere. The terms *casting* and *raising* will be used interchangeably in this book.

Casting a Basic Circle

Casting a circle is straightforward. Although Wicca 101 books offer endless variations upon it, the following are the basic steps involved.

What to Do:

1. Stand in the center of the space you will define as your circle.
2. Extend your projective hand outward to where the circle wall will be. (Your projective hand is the hand you send energy out with—as opposed to your receptive hand. Often, your projective hand is your dominant hand, but don't let this generalization trap you into using only your right hand if you're right-handed, or vice versa.)
3. Center your personal energy, then ground it into the energy of the earth below.
4. With your projective hand still extended, draw energy up from the earth through your grounded connection, and allow it to flow out through your hand.
5. Turning clockwise, allow that energy to flow into the space around you where you desire your circle to form. Turn around completely until you are again facing the original starting point and the flow of energy meets up with where it was started.
6. Allow the two ends to merge together to create a seamless ring of energy around you, and then visualize the ring

thickening and curving inward until it meets above your head and below your feet.

7. Drop your hand to shut off the energy flow you have been drawing on.

Variations on Circle-Creation Techniques

Experiment with these variations on the basic way to create a circle. You may surprise yourself with how well you click with one method or another.

One very simple variation involves programming the energy you use. When you channel the energy to lie around your perimeter, you can program it. Programming is basically tinting the energy you're channeling with a purpose or intent. When you raise a basic circle, you most likely usually think of protection. If you're raising a circle in order to perform a healing ritual, however, you may wish to program the circle for protection and health.

As an intermediate Wiccan, you will no doubt be seeking ways to vary your circle-casting routine (dismantling variations will be explored later in this chapter). Following, you will find some thought-provoking questions. You can use the answers supplied to enact your variations, or simply use the questions as a guide to challenge yourself to find ways to change your basic circle-cast.

Do You Need to Cleanse, Purify, and Consecrate Before Raising a Circle for Ritual?

Some Wiccans believe that you must always cleanse, purify, and consecrate the space where you will construct your circle. Others believe that cleansing and purifying is necessary, but that the act of creating the circle constitutes consecration of the space. Still others believe that it is not necessary at all to prepare the space in any way before you raise your circle.

After more than a decade of trying it all three ways my personal belief is that it's important psychologically to engage in the steps of cleansing (personal and of the area) and purification, but not necessarily the steps of consecration, before raising a circle. These first two steps help you get into the correct mental state for ritual. The physical acts of tidying, washing, and preparing the space reinforce the respect you hold for the act you are about to perform, and they reduce the amount of visual distraction around you. The purification removes any remaining distracting energy as well. Ignoring these first two steps is like skipping the warm-up before a workout. As with exercise, if you mentally and physically prepare yourself before engaging in the activity, your results will be that much better.

Are Tools Necessary to Cast a Circle?

If you've always used a tool to aid you in casting a circle, it's time to put it down on the altar and give casting with your bare hands a try. Conversely, if you've always used your hands, try casting with a tool. The most popular tools for raising a circle are the wand, the athame, the staff, and the sword. While a ritual sword can be useful in groups because it can be easily seen, there are not that many benefits to using a big, clunky sword when you're working alone. If you feel like experimenting, try casting with a stone or crystal of some kind (stones with projective energies work best; receptive energies don't channel energy out as well), a flower, or a wand made of various greenery tied together like a sage smudge.

Must You Always Raise a Circle Deasil?

Most books tell beginner Wiccans that a circle should *always* be cast *deasil* (clockwise) and unspun *widdershins* (counterclockwise). As a result, most beginners get it into their heads that it's evil or wrong to cast a circle counterclockwise, and that moving counterclockwise is evil, period.

There are a variety of ritual purposes that a counterclockwise cast may suit, including dark moon esbats, banishing rituals, and rituals wherein you aspect a dark goddess or god (see Chapter Eleven for a discussion of dark deities). You don't necessarily draw on evil, murky, corruptive energy when you cast counterclockwise. You know that light and dark, as well as positive and negative, don't have value judgments attached to them. The same applies to moving clockwise or counterclockwise. The direction stirs a specific sort of energy, but how you use that energy is always up to you. If you have never cast a circle counterclockwise, try it at least once, preferably three times, and record your experiences.

The one rule to keep in mind is that if you raise your circle by moving and stirring energy counterclockwise, then all your movements in your ritual must also be counterclockwise: your quarter-calls, any procession you may make, and so forth (except for your dismissal, of course). This can be a bit counterintuitive if you've always worked clockwise before. You will really have to concentrate when you first try this, but work through it to the end and then make notes in your book of shadows as to how you feel. As you advance, you may surprise yourself with how easily you handle techniques such as this.

Does the Size of the Circle Matter?

The size of the circle you cast depends on what you're going to do in it and on your frame of mind. Some clever practitioners (my husband included) will cast their circles to the walls to include everything in the room and to have plenty of space to move around. There's an additional benefit to casting a circle to the walls of the room: if you discover that you have forgotten something and it's in the room, you can just walk over and pick it up. If you're used to casting big circles, challenge yourself to cast a smaller one to get comfortable with using energy in a tighter environment.

Many prefer the more intimate feeling of a circle approximately six feet in diameter. If you're one of those who prefer a small circle, practice raising large circles once in a while, just so you can get used to the feeling of it. Some rituals call for a lot of movement, and you'll have to be knowledgeable about casting a larger circle to accommodate your motion.

Do You Need Both Words and Physical Motion When Casting a Circle?

Circle-casting is a combination of visualization, power of will, belief, and energy channeling. Like certain physical actions, words can trigger unconscious responses and ease us into a transition, but in the end words are really as unnecessary as physical actions. A circle-cast can be as quiet and as simple as this:

1. Create a small ball of white or blue light in your energy center, usually located around your solar plexus.
2. Slowly and steadily expand this ball outward until it has formed a sphere the size you require.

With strong visualization and channeling of the earth's energy, this can sometimes be enough, but it's best to now walk this circle once to solidify it. Physical actions are often included to engage the conscious mind and to reinforce the defined space. But physical motion is simply another form of energy, so if you don't wish to use it, you don't need to.

For more ideas on how to work with energy alone in an advanced fashion, see Chapter Eleven, which addresses inner temples and performing ritual entirely on the astral level, with no physical involvement at all.

Intermediate Circle-Casting Techniques

Having thought about the previous questions, you will now be ready to formulate your own intermediate circle-raising technique. Try the following techniques if you'd like to experiment before creating your own.

Variations on the Single Pass Circle

To vary the basic technique of walking the perimeter of your circle area a single time, channeling energy into the barrier, use different-colored energy. Match the energy's color and programming to whatever your ritual purpose may be. Visualizing color adds the energy of the color to your circle; it's a different method of programming it, as each color carries corresponding energies. For example, you can use green energy for healing, blue for justice rituals, or an appropriate sabbat-associated color for whatever sabbat you may be celebrating. Many Wiccans prefer to use white energy, silver energy, or blue energy. These three colors are multipurpose and correspond to protection and peace.

Variations on the Three-Fold Pass Circle

Another common method practiced by Wiccans involves walking the circle perimeter three times, as three is recognized as a sacred number:

1. Walk your circle perimeter three times, casting one layer of the circle by channeling energy as per your usual method, then channel a second just inside the first, and then a third just inside the second.
2. When you are done, stand and concentrate, visualizing all three layers merging into one.

There are many ways to vary the three-fold circle:

- You can allow each layer to grow up and into the sphere shape, remaining separated from the other two. This will give you three distinct barriers that together form your sacred circle.
- You can cast in the names of the triple-aspected deities of Wicca, if you like, or for the triple layers of reality perceived by various cultures (the underworld, the material world, and the spiritual overworld).
- You can cast each layer while visualizing a different color of energy emerging from your hand or tool. When you've finished your third layer, you can visualize all three different-colored layers coming together to form a multicolored energy barrier.

Triple Axis Circle

A very different form of the three-fold pass is known as the triple axis circle. While it may be hard to visualize casting a circle in three dimensions, it's remarkably easy to do in practice. If you feel unsure after reading the steps, walk yourself through them without channeling energy. This method reinforces the idea of the barrier existing above, below, and behind the Wiccan inside it.

What to Do:

1. Cast your first circle around you parallel to the floor. This will be your *x*-axis. Do not visualize the rim of the circle growing up into a sphere; leave it as a ring of energy around you.

2. From your starting and ending point, cast your second circle by moving your hand directly up and arcing toward you. Continue the arc up, over your head, and turn as you follow it down (you'll be across from your starting point). Follow the arc (now a half-circle) down under your feet, and up to meet the point of origin once again. This will be your *y*-axis.

3. Finally, make a quarter-turn to your right so that your point of origin for the first two circles is directly to your left. Extend your hand to touch the energy of the first circle and connect the starting point of your third circle to the existing first circle. Draw the third circle from that starting point, up and over your head. You will touch (intersect) the arc of your second circle directly above your head. Next, move your hand down to touch the rim of the first circle on the side opposite the third circle's origin point, and then move your hand down under your feet to connect again with the

second circle. Continue your arc upward to meet the rim of the first circle and the third circle's point of origin again. This is your z-axis.

4. You will now be standing within an energy cage of sorts. Visualize the three circles blending into a perfect sphere.

An Elemental Energy Four-Fold Pass Circle

A four-fold pass honors the four physical elements and creates a different sort of balanced energy within the circle. If you enjoy working with elemental energy, this casting technique may resonate well with you.

As you did in the basic three-fold pass, create separate circles— each inside the other, one by one—but in this exercise you will cast a fourth circle on the inside so that it lies within the first three. As you cast each circle, focus on channeling the energy of a different element. You may choose to begin with air and end with earth, symbolizing the evolution from thought to action, or inspiration to manifestation. Or you may begin and end with the order of whichever elements you feel drawn to.

You can visualize the four circles blending into one, and see that mergence as the manifestation of Spirit, the fifth element, from the four physical elements. If you choose to combine these four circles, do so with care. If you are unused to handling elemental energy, merging them may be tricky for you. Be sure to cast all four circles with equal intensity, or the merging will be uneven and your circle will be dominated by one kind of energy instead of providing a balance of all four.

Within the Circle

Raising a circle is usually the first step within standard Wiccan ritual (unless, of course, you've used sacred space instead). It's often followed by the step commonly referred to as calling the quarters, or the invocation of the elemental energies to be present. Finally, deity is invoked. With these steps complete, Wiccan ritual is then ready for whatever purpose you require—the celebration of a sabbat or esbat, the casting of a spell, meditation, aspecting, or any number of acts.

How Do You Create a Door in the Circle?

One of the most important things you must do within a circle is cut a door if you need to pass through the boundary. Why must you create a door through which to pass? If you walk through the energy wall, you weaken your own perception and belief in the curved barrier between the worlds that you have created. By weakening this perception, you also add support to the idea usually lurking in the back of your mind that the barrier doesn't really exist, and this traitorous idea further sabotages your energy-handling ability.

Very advanced practitioners can sometimes attune to their circles to such a point that they can meld their energy with that of the circle, step through as if through a waterfall, and detach their energy on the other side. This doesn't weaken the energy barrier, but it does nothing to reinforce the idea of the circle as a defined space. It's a difficult thing to do, and takes a lot of practice, often with a friend who stays inside the circle to see if the circle changes at all after you pass through it. You can practice it, but it's often a better idea to use a more traditional method of cutting a door.

Cutting a Door in Your Circle with a Tool

What to Do:

1. Take your wand or athame and insert it into the energy wall where it intersects the floor with the intent of creating an egress.
2. Pull the tip of the tool up to a few inches past your head height. Pull it across through the wall about three feet, then draw the tip of the tool downward to the floor again.
3. Lay the tool on the floor with the tip outside the circle and the handle inside. This anchors both the circle and your doorway.
4. Step through the doorframe you have just cut and get what you need quickly and calmly.
5. Return to your circle and step back through the door.
6. Pick up your tool and carefully retrace the edges of the door, visualizing the cut you made sealing up again. Some practitioners like to walk the perimeter of the circle once in a clockwise direction, just to ensure that the correct flow of the circle's energy has been restored.

Cutting a Door in Your Circle Without a Tool

What to Do:

1. Hold your hands out in front of you, palms together. Slowly insert them into the energy of your circle, willing it to accept your own energy.

2. Carefully pull your hands apart and visualize the wall of energy parting like a pair of curtains.

3. Step through and allow the energy curtains to fall shut behind you. Get what you need quickly and calmly, then return to the circle and perform the same action from the outside.

4. After you have stepped through, smooth the energy curtains back into the wall of the circle. Again, you may wish to walk the perimeter of the circle, trailing your hand along the energy barrier to restore the correct flow that may have been interrupted by your passage.

What's this about a "correct flow"? A circle isn't a static object. When you raise it, you don't cement energy into place. Energy is constantly moving, and when you use it to form a circle it flows in the direction (usually clockwise) in which you cast it.

Dismantling a Basic Circle

Dismantling the circle is just as important as raising it! Unlike sacred space, which slowly fades over time, a circle must be taken down with as much attention and respect as you used to raise it. All steps must be done with reverence, closing the ritual with the same degree of ceremony as you observed when you entered into it.

There are negative repercussions if you don't take down your circle. First, you'll have to walk through the barrier to get out of the defined area. As in failing to create a door, this act sabotages your belief in that barrier. Walking through a circle throws your own personal energy out of balance. It can also "pop" the circle, which will release any energy within it in an uncontrolled fashion.

If you haven't dealt with the energy inside the circle, a sudden release can psychically harm you or those around you.

Basic Dismantling Method

The basic method of taking down any circle is to fundamentally do the reverse of the basic circle-cast.

What to Do:

1. Stand in the center of your circle and extend your receptive hand out toward the wall of the circle. Center your personal energy, then ground it into the energy of the earth below.
2. With your receptive hand extended, begin to draw the energy of the circle into your hand and down into the earth. Turning counterclockwise, allow the energy of the circle to flow into your hand and down to the earth until you face your original starting point and the energy of the circle is all gone.
3. Drop your hand, shutting off the energy flow, and disconnect from the earth. Your hand may feel tingly or odd after collecting the energy—shake it a few times to get rid of the last traces of the circle energy that may be clinging to it. Center yourself again, and ground once more.
4. If you have accidentally sent some of your own energy away into the earth with the circle energy, draw back what you need to equalize. If you still have energy remaining in your system that shouldn't be there, let it flow down to join the energy of the earth until you are balanced again.

Variations on Circle-Dismantling Techniques

Dismantling your circle does not necessarily mean repeating the multiple steps of casting it in reverse order. Dismantling tends to be less complex than raising. It is sufficient to dismantle the circle as if it consisted of one layer. Most Wiccans formulate their own personal method of respectfully dismantling their circles.

The Demi-Circle Split Dismissal

This dismissal can be difficult at first, because you don't allow the energy to flow into you and then into the ground. Instead, you direct the energy into the earth by pushing it gently. It may take a bit of practice if you are used to channeling energy through you instead of handling it outside yourself.

What to Do:

1. Stand in the center of your circle and bring your hands up over your head so that your fingers and palms touch. Then turn your hands so that they are back to back.
2. Center and ground, and breathe deeply a couple of times. Sense the energy extending from your fingers gently inserting itself into the curved roof of your circle.
3. Slowly begin to lower your hands, keeping your arms straight. As you do, visualize a seam opening within the circle; the seam is aligned with your fingertips, so that the circle separates gently along the top, front, and back.
4. With your hands still moving steadily, lower each half of the circle, visualizing the energy flowing into the ground until your hands are at your sides and all the circle's energy

is gone. (Don't forget to visualize the section of the circle under your feet being absorbed into the ground as well.)

Channeling Circle Energy Into an Object Rather Than the Ground

This method stores the energy in a tool for future use.

What to Do:

1. Choose a tool to serve as the object of the channeling. People often like to use something active, such as a wand or athame. You could choose to use your altar.

2. If you can, hold the tool in front of you with both hands. Center, then ground. Reach out and touch the tool to the energy of the circle and visualize the energy being drawn into the tool. Do not visualize the energy carrying through the tool to your hands. You may stand in one place and allow the tool to draw in the energy until it is gone, or you may walk counterclockwise and gather the energy with the tool.

3. If you cannot hold the tool or if it is too awkward to handle, place your projective hand upon the tool and reach up with your receptive hand. Visualize the energy of the circle being drawn down into your receptive hand, through your arm, down your other arm, and into the tool. In this case, as in the basic dismantling method, you are serving as a channel through which the energy of the circle travels, and nothing more.

4. No foreign energy should remain in you when you are finished. If it does, disengage from the tool, shake your

hands in the air as if you were flipping off water, and center and ground again. If you have excess energy, allow it to flow away from you into the earth.

5. If you've mistakenly put some of your own energy into the tool, then draw some energy up from the earth to rebalance yourself.

Chapter Four

Spells and Energy Work

Although the basic tenets of Wicca do not include the practice of magic and spellcraft, most Wiccans do incorporate it into their practice to some degree. In this chapter we will examine the structure of spellcraft and the energy-handling techniques involved.

What Is a Spell?

Spellwork seeks to alter a situation by introducing new energy or rearranging the energy already present in a situation. You perform a spell with intent and awareness to create change. Spells involve sequential symbolic actions performed in the physical world to initialize change on another level.

Spellwork may take place within a ritual framework, but the spell itself is not a ritual. A ritual celebrates, honors, or initializes spiritual change in a religious context, while a spell is an active method of using energy to power some sort of change. (A spell can certainly take place in a spiritual context, of course; we'll get to that in a minute.)

Spells aren't prayers, even though Wiccans and non-Wiccans alike sometimes describe them as such. Praying is a religious act, whereas the art of crafting and casting a spell is secular. Prayer appeals to a higher power for aid in some fashion; with a spell *you* are the agent of change. You call upon your own resources to gather and direct energy instead of employing a separate agent, such as a higher power, to accomplish the task. A spell is not more powerful or more successful than a prayer, nor is the inverse true.

Not all spellcasters are Wiccan, despite the masses of spell books that include pseudo-Wiccan framework and that invoke deity as standard operating procedure. As you read in Chapter One, Wicca has become the most recognizable form of neo-Pagan practice, and it's not surprising that the Wiccan approach to spells has filtered into the popular mind as the "right" or "only" way to perform spells.

In my book *Power Spellcraft for Life* I separated spells from spirituality. In this book we will examine the two concepts together.

As Wicca seeks to inform every facet of your life, it makes sense to incorporate your spirituality into your spellcraft.

Why Wiccans Cast Spells

Spellcasting certainly isn't the sole reason for practicing Wicca, but it dovetails nicely with your spiritual practice. As Wiccans, we are concerned with improving ourselves and, by extension, improving the world. Crafting and casting spells help in both of these areas. Spells offer a method for actively dealing with situations in life that require an additional boost of energy, and also offer an opportunity to maintain or restore balance. Spells are catalysts for change.

When a Wiccan casts a spell, a deity is very often brought into that method of powering change. This creates an interesting form of spiritual spellcraft that merges the basic secular spell, often being seen as an act of prayer or appeal to deity to lend aid. Wiccan spellcraft, like other forms of religious spellcraft, adds a ritual dimension to spells, making it much more than simple witchcraft.

The very processes of crafting and casting spells teach you the basics of energy work—whether you realize it or not. Spells teach you how energy moves, how you can harness and handle it, and how you can direct it to affect various areas of your life. Whereas rituals offer you the opportunity to tap into the energy around you to re-attune yourself on a regular basis, spells allow you to touch the web of energy that connects those living and organic things day by day, and to see how touching it in a slightly different place produces a slightly different effect.

How Spells Work

Everything in the world emits an energy vibration of some kind, with different things having different energy signatures. Sometimes a signature is referred to as possessing a different *level* of vibration. A higher level is usually considered more spiritual and closer to the gods; a lower vibration indicates something more material. These energies reach out to touch one another, forming what amounts to a giant spider web of energy that crisscrosses around the world. It also connects the physical and nonphysical worlds. (This is often referred to as "the web.")

As everything is connected in this fashion, it is possible to have an effect on things simply by twitching the web in one place and allowing the resulting vibration to flow along the web until it reaches your goal. The web is also how we can send energy to someone or something far away from us—the strands of energy that connect all organic and living things serve as wires through which we can send our energy.

The Basic Steps in Spellcraft

As in crafting rituals, creating and casting a spell follow a certain sequence of events. While every spell is different, the basic steps are:

1. **Establish your need or desire.** Doing a spell for the sake of doing a spell is a waste of time and energy. Why trouble the web and the pattern of energy around you if you don't have to?
2. **Compose your spell.** It is essential to determine a clear and precisely defined goal. Take the time to think about your desired outcome. Think, too, about the energies you wish to incorporate or call upon to help you achieve that goal.

3. **Shift consciousness.** Your mind must be in the correct mode for working spells. A mind overrun by everyday thoughts isn't very efficient at gathering energies, weaving them into a tight and well-focused spell, and then releasing them toward a goal. Shifting your consciousness allows you to attain a different state of mind ideal for ritual or spellcraft. You need to be able to filter out the surface noise and distractions to concentrate and focus on what you're doing. (This state is often referred to as *alpha*, which indicates the frequency of brain waves associated with wakeful relaxation, an ideal state in which to do ritual or magic.)

4. **Raise energy and release it toward your goal.** Spells are powered by the energies possessed by the correspondences you incorporate in your spells as well as your own personal energy.

5. **Manifest.** Ideally, the final step is the achievement of your goal.

Basic Energy-Working Skills

If you practice Wicca alone, it can be frustrating to read about energy handling and not know if you're doing it right, or if you're even doing it at all. You may feel unsure about what you are supposed to see and feel and what is supposed to happen. If you work with a group, you may find that the way people sense energy is so different that your descriptive language may not match up, which can lead to self-doubt.

The creation of sacred space (explored in Chapter Two) and casting a circle (explored in Chapter Three) both use some of the basic skills that most Wiccans develop through intuitive use and practice. Examining the basics once you've reached an intermediate to advanced level can be useful in that it gives you new insight into why or how you do things as well as how others experience them, and more confidence in how you do what you do. The following sections will outline the three basic skills found in working with energy, examine some common problems associated with the techniques, and suggest ways to overcome obstacles.

Centering

The term *centering* describes the process of focusing on the spiritual and energy center of your body. Centering is usually paired with grounding as a prelude to spellwork or ritual. Oddly enough, the common phrase "grounding and centering" is often used, suggesting that you ought to ground before you center. Many people do this, but I find that the reverse is more helpful. You need a place within yourself from which to begin the grounding process. It makes less sense to reach outside yourself to try to grab earth energy and then use it to pinpoint your center.

Centering helps focus you. Centering also collects the bits of stray personal energy that are diffused throughout your body and personal aura, and it draws them back to your personal power place in your energy center. Your personal energy becomes *centered*. Think of it as coiling a spring before you release it—you increase the potential energy of the spring by compressing it.

Centering is a slippery term and this can be frustrating. What on earth is your energy center, and how do you find it? Beginner books describe the center in attractive but somewhat vague terms:

> *The process of focusing on your spiritual center, allowing all mundane issues to fall away leaving calm and serenity.* (Buckland, p. 233)

To find the ultimate, peaceful calm at the center of your being...the still point—the absolute moment of calm when you feel like you are one with the universe. (RavenWolf, *Solitary Witch,* p. 238)

Passages such as these describe the *feeling* you get when you have centered. But how do you figure out where your spiritual and energy center is? Ask yourself the following questions:

- From where do you instinctively sense your personal energy emanating?
- Where do you first feel emotion?
- Where do you first sense energy, or experience intuitive sensations?
- When you raise energy, is there a point in your body that resonates with it?
- If you relax and allow your awareness to examine different areas within your body, what feels most like a repository of energy?

Most people find that their center is a chakra point (one of the seven major energy nodes in the spiritual body, which overlaps the physical body). For many people the center is the solar plexus. This is an instinctive association because the solar plexus is the approximate center of our physical form. The second most common place for your center is the third eye, or the brow chakra, located in the center of the forehead. This center can be a bit more challenging to work with. People tend to unconsciously tense up the physical muscles around their center when they work with it. If you get frequent headaches when you work with energy, it may be because your center is located at your brow chakra.

Grounding

Think of a three-pronged electrical plug, which has the third prong in it to help protect you or an appliance against excess electricity if it surges, by shunting excess power away from the outlet into a grounding wire. Grounding your personal energy is a similar concept.

Grounding has many benefits. It renders you physically sturdier and more aware of your environment. If you are naturally jumpy or nervous, ground frequently and observe the effect upon your state of mind and your physical status.

When doing energy work of any kind, you should always maintain an energy connection to the earth so that you can safely shunt excess energy away from your own energy center. This avoids an overflow of energy in your closed system, which can lead to the system shorting out. Overloading yourself with excess energy can be quite disorienting, and in extreme cases it can be harmful. An imbalance of energy, be it an excess or a lack, is never ideal. Too many people use just their own personal energy to power spells or rituals, even when they believe they're using energy gained from elsewhere. As a result, they end up tired, ill, and with their personal energy seriously unbalanced, which can further affect mental performance and emotional reactions. Gripping the muscles around your center too tightly isn't the only cause of headaches while working with energy or performing ritual. This type of feeling can also be related to how you're grounded, or how your energy is connected to the energy of the earth.

There is an immense amount of energy lying within the earth, and proper grounding allows you to draw upon this reserve. Some people say that they feel selfish or that it's unfair to take energy from the earth; they feel as if they are cheating somehow. Nothing could be farther from the truth. The trace amounts that you may draw upon from the earth make little to no difference to that vast store. Remember, too, that when you ground to release excess energy, you are putting energy back into the earth. It all evens out in the long run.

The earth is a great neutralizer. No matter what flavor of energy you deposit into it, the energy you draw up will always be pure and untainted. One of the best ways to cleanse a stone or a tool of previous energy it may have collected is to bury it, in either salt or soil. Earth absorbs negative energy, rendering it neutral and safe for future use.

As a quick review: You do not have to be physically standing *on* the ground in order to ground your energy. You can do it in a moving vehicle; you can do it in a high-rise apartment, in an airplane, or on a ship. The central core of the earth is omnipresent. Simply think down, and allow your energy to sink downward until you feel it connect to the energy of the earth. Depending on how you sense energy, you may not have to go down very far before you connect with it. You may not even have to reach the surface of the earth, for instance. Different people have different comfort levels. Some may feel secure grounding close to the surface, while others may prefer to sink deep into the earth. Experiment and ascertain your optimal grounded sensation.

Basic Grounding

This is a version of a basic grounding meditation.

What to Do:

1. Center your energy. Imagine a seed of light within your energy center.
2. Visualize that seed sprouting a tendril of energy, which proceeds to grow downward through your body. Sometimes this tendril extends directly downward from the base of your spine into the ground, and sometimes it divides into two tendrils to flow down your legs and into the ground through your feet. Once in the ground, that tendril thickens and expands, growing downward even farther, until you sense that it has joined with the energy deep within the earth. If you wish, you can further envision the tendril splitting into roots that absorb energy.
3. Once this connection to the earth is established, the tendril will draw energy up to you and your center to power your work. And with this same connection you may allow excess energy, or energy you collect from your environment, to flow down to join the earth's energy.

Grounding Up

There are more ways to ground than just visualizing the standard roots. If you cannot visualize sinking your personal energy line into the ground, try grounding up. For remarkable steadiness, ground both down and up. This sort of connection creates a column-like stability that makes you difficult to unbalance.

What to Do:

1. Visualize the same tendril of light extending from your energy center, but allow it to reach up instead of down. Allow it to rise up into the sky until you sense it connecting with the energy of the sun, the moon, or the stars.
2. Rebalance your energy as you require when using this connection.

Channeling Energy

Think of a wire that connects a battery to a light bulb. When the end of the wire touches the battery's node and the circuit is closed, the electricity flows from the battery to the light bulb and the light goes on. When the wire's end is removed from the battery, the flow of the energy current is broken, and the light goes off. Channeling energy is a similar process. When you channel, you become the wire that connects an energy source to something in need of energy. The energy passes through you without harming you, just as the current passes through the wire without destroying the wire.

There are other ways to channel energy. Unlike the wire, you have a source of energy within you: your will and your spiritual energy body. This is one of the reasons for grounding. Once you have grounded, you have established a connection with a huge energy source upon which you can safely draw without depleting your own energy reserve.

The term *channeling* can also apply to being a passive conduit for other information or energy to pass through (as in the idea of channeling a deity). This aspect of channeling is addressed in Chapter Twelve.

Channeling is an energy exercise that people tend to make more difficult than it actually is. Many people believe they must somehow *push* the energy to channel it—the result is tension, and often a headache. The only effort required lies in the act of relaxing and allowing the energy to flow. Allowing yourself to relax can be a remarkably challenging act. If you relax, particularly to channel energy, you may feel as if you are giving up control in some way. This is false, however: when you channel, you remain completely aware of what is happening, and can stop at any time.

Sensing Energy

Always trust yourself when you are working with energy. It's all too easy to doubt what you're doing. You may wonder: If I channel, am I really filling an object with the energy I think I'm channeling? If I invoke a deity, am I really sensing their presence? When I call a quarter, am I truly opening my space to the archetypal energy of that element? You can hone your energy-sensing skills so that you will be able to better sense any shift or change. You need to create and practice your own methods of sensing energy—and of recognizing that you're doing it.

Energy-Sensing Exercise

Use the following technique to help you gain confidence in your energy-sensing abilities.

What to Do:

1. Center and ground. From your energy center extend a tendril of energy along your arm to your hand, and then allow it to gather slightly around your hand like a mitten or a glove, or to gather along your palm and your fingers. Reach toward the object you wish to sense. Do not physically touch it. Instead, let that layer of your personal energy encounter the object. With your personal energy explore the object's energy. What do you sense? When reading and sensing energy, your interpretation of information will be unique. Energy information may include a sense of warmth or coolness, various degrees of tingling, a sense of being drawn toward the object or pushed away from it, or a sense of color evoked from the energy.

2. Run your hands around the object without touching it physically, feeling the energy it possesses. What do you sense? How is this different from actively employing your energy to sense the energy of the object?

3. Play with the distance. Instead of covering your palm and fingers with the energy from your center, extend it farther and sense objects at a distance. Remember to keep the energy extension focused. Don't let it broaden too much; control is necessary. Practice extending and reabsorbing this energy tendril used to sense objects until you become comfortable with it. Be careful not to completely meld your energy with the energy of the object

you are sensing. You are not attempting to channel or draw the other energy into you; you are simply "tasting" the energy.

4. Always remember to keep detailed notes on your efforts and results in your book of shadows. These notes will reassure you when you have a crisis of faith in yourself and your abilities. Going back to them can help you explore the various ways in which you react to different energies, and how your abilities fluctuate with your mood, your health, and the kinds of objects you sense.

Chapter Five

Simple Rituals

The structures of simple rituals such as purification, consecration, and blessing are examined in this chapter.

Simple Ritual Basics

Simple rituals are some of the building blocks used in larger, more complex rituals. You've already read about the steps essential to the creation of sacred space (cleansing, purification, and consecration), and these same steps appear again for crafting other rituals. These simple rituals are also used on their own as necessary.

> Note that simple rituals do not include creating sacred space or raising a circle, or calling quarters, or invoking deity. That's all part of your ritual framework, and we'll look at it in Chapter Seven.

A smaller ritual within a larger ritual is often referred to as a *rite*. Thus, the simple rituals in this chapter may be referred to as rites of banishing, rites of purification, and so forth.

Some of these steps will be familiar to you because you already do them. Many Wiccans combine steps and do more than one at once. It's important to separate the steps and look at each distinct one to completely understand what is at work. The most common simple rituals are:

- Purifying
- Banishing
- Consecrating
- Dedicating
- Blessing

It is not uncommon to see two or more simple rituals linked together. If you banish something, chances are good that you will follow it directly with a blessing to fill up the empty space you have created. Nature abhors a vacuum, after all, and to remove the negative energy of a space or an object does not necessarily mean that positive energy will immediately flow to fill that void.

Many books use some of these terms interchangeably, which can make things very confusing. Also, the simple rituals in most books tend to be parts of larger, more elaborate rituals, and difficult to extract for use on their own. As in the chapter on creating sacred space, let's look at each of these rites separately to gain a deeper understanding of what they entail. Let's examine the terms first, and then move into some sample rites.

Purifying

To purify something is to remove any previous non-innate energy that may be present. The act of purification can never remove the native properties of something. To purify an object is to return it to its original untainted or unaltered state.

Some Wiccans refer to purification as *exorcism*, which implies that there is something negative attached to the object. *Exorcism* is a word better suited to the actual removal of something confirmed as actively negative. On a day-to-day level *purification* is a more appropriate term to use.

Banishing

To banish something is to send it away. There are various usages of this term throughout Wicca, and it's important to understand exactly who and/or what is being banished when you use the term.

In some Wiccan literature the act of taking down a circle is sometimes referred to as "banishing" it. When you banish a circle, you are dispersing the energy associated with it. Usage of the word *banishing* implies that you are literally sending the energy of the circle elsewhere; you are not channeling it into a tool for future use, nor are you absorbing it into yourself to then channel into the ground. You may be uncomfortable with this use of the term, especially if you feel that you dismantle your circle with the same love you used to raise it. This is a good example of how terms in Wicca become ingrained, without the practitioner pausing to consider what sort of imagery may be accompanying the term.

Most commonly "banishing" suggests a forced removal of actively negative energy, like an exorcism. In this usage you would banish a spirit or persistent negative energy. To banish something in this way is to assert your authority over it, and to command it to depart. Sometimes people use the word *banish* in purification rituals. In other words, they "banish all negativity" from an item before proceeding according to their purpose. Depending on what that purpose is, the term can be a bit strong for what they're actually doing.

Additionally, a person can be banished, or sent into some form of exile. This usage of the word usually applies to groups or communities and indicates someone who has seriously damaged the group or trespassed in some unforgivable way. Sometimes banishment can be used as a means to preserve peace.

Consecrating

Consecration is a two-fold process. It purifies, and it instills or creates a connection between the object and its new sanctity. As in the regular simple ritual of purifying, the first part of the act of consecration removes any previous non-innate energy that may be present. As in the rite of purification, you can never remove the innate, native properties of something by consecrating it. Consecration usually focuses on removing any negative energy that may have collected around the object. This serves a dual purpose: first, it removes any impediment to the object's natural energy; second, it "produce[s] a psychological effect on the user that strengthens confidence in the object's ability to accomplish its intended task while validating its sanctity" (Wilborn, p. 129). In eclectic Wicca the phrase "cleanse and consecrate" is often used, but this is somewhat redundant because it indicates the two-fold process already included in the very definition of consecration.

Consecration also has the added bonus of aligning your purpose within the ritual with the object's purpose within the ritual. In regular jargon the word *consecrate* means to make sacred, and that's partially what happens in a rite of consecration. Something is consecrated or sealed *to* a purpose or a deity, confirming its suitability for use within a religious ritual.

Consecrating the Elements

Consecration is often used upon the elements before they are employed in ritual. This basic rite of consecration uses the example of a small bowl of salt representing the element of earth. Two versions of the spoken words are provided here as an example, and in the second the two steps in the rite are more clearly separated. First, the salt is purified of anything not naturally connected with it. Second, the physical representation (the salt) is connected to the spiritual equivalent, the archetype of earth.

What to Do:

Holding your hands over the bowl, or touching the salt, say:

O creature of earth,
I cleanse and consecrate you
to remove all negativity and imperfection in the world both seen
and unseen.
Be for me the sacred element of earth.
So mote it be.

This is the alternate:

O creature of earth,
I purify you
To remove all negativity in the world both seen and unseen.
I consecrate you as the sacred element of earth.
So mote it be.

Consecrate any component or supply you bring to a ritual or spell, and the energy that item brings to your work will be purer and flow freer. Here is an example of a basic ingredient or supply consecration. In it the item is purified and consecrated to its use in the names of the Wiccan deities. Once the elements have been consecrated, they are ready to be used in further rites of consecration, or in a rite of dedication:

I cleanse and consecrate this candle in the name of the Lord and
the Lady,
That it be for me a fit tool by which to [state your intention or
the purpose of the object].
So mote it be.

Should you consecrate something anew each time you do ritual? It depends on the object. Elements should always be consecrated before use, even if you're using the same candle to represent the element of fire, or the same bowl of salt, sand, or earth to represent the element of earth. Generally, something consumable or meant for a single use is consecrated; something permanent is dedicated.

Dedicating

Similar to a consecration, a dedication clears away old or non-innate energy from an object, person, or space, and seals it to a new action or use. A dedication suggests a new beginning or a new life for the person, item, or space, whereas consecration initializes an item but does not actively set it in motion. To dedicate a person means to seal the person to a purpose or a path. This can be done to welcome a new person into an existing group; solitary practitioners who wish to make a formal recognition of the spiritual path they have chosen to follow may perform a version of self-dedication.

Dedication instills or creates a connection between the object/space/person and practitioner in a way that consecration does not. The act of dedicating creates a more permanent connection, although it can be undone: an object dedicated to a specific purpose remains dedicated to that purpose until you specify otherwise.

Dedicating a space involves programming or charging it with a specific purpose. A circle, for example, is often cast with words, such as:

> *I cast you, my circle,*
> *To be a space between this world and the next,*
> *To be a space of love and trust*

Where I will worship the Lord and the Lady,
And to contain the power I raise inside.

This wording indicates that you are dedicating your space to four different things: to being a place between the worlds; to being a space filled with love and trust; to being a place of worship of specific deities; and to being a container for the energy with which you'll be working.

To dedicate an object means that you're ritually sealing it to one purpose. A tool dedication clears old energy away from the item you intend to use in a ritual context, leaving a clean slate for you to imbue with the energy you desire to associate with it. One of the most common dedication rites a Wiccan engages in is a tool dedication.

Tool Dedication

A common method of dedicating a tool is to purify it by the four elements (already consecrated), as in the following example.

What You Need:

- Tool to be dedicated
- Incense in censer
- Matches or a lighter
- Candle in holder
- Small cup or bowl of water
- Small cup or bowl of salt

What to Do:

Hold the tool in your hands, or place your hands upon or above it, and say:

O [tool],
I purify you by air [pass the tool through incense smoke];
I purify you by fire [pass the tool through the flame of a candle
or through the light it casts];
I purify you by water [sprinkle a few drops of water on the tool];
I purify you by earth [touch the tool to the salt].
I charge you to serve me well within the sacred circle,
And I dedicate you to deepening my practice of the ways of
Wicca.

The last two lines dedicate the tool to two purposes: to aid you and to enhance your spiritual practice.

Blessing

A blessing is an active request for positive energy to touch an item or person. For Wiccans this also means asking for the grace of the Divine in the name of the Goddess and/or God. If you work with a specific god-form (or god-forms), you will most likely bless in their names. As you know and work closely with them, you can thus accurately represent their energy as being active and present in the communication of the blessing.

Blessing is often the rite that caps another rite, for it invites positive energy into the area, object, or person that already has been cleansed and purified of negative energy. You can bless someone or something with general positive energy, or you can channel something more specific, such as a blessing for health or for prosperity. In the Wiccan celebratory ritual of cakes and wine the food and beverage are consecrated and then blessed with the energy of the Divine. They are then consumed so that the blessing is internalized.

Sometimes a blessing is given in a fashion similar to a dedication—by each element. In this instance you are asking for the blessings of each element, or for the associated archetypal energy to touch the object of the blessing. When this is done, a blessing is usually also asked of Spirit, the fifth element, and is done by either the laying on of hands, the ringing of a bell, or anointment with a consecrated oil.

Sample Ritual

The following is a suggested outline of a consecration ceremony for a spiritual journal. It uses several of the simple rites outlined in this chapter.

Sample Ritual to Dedicate a Book of Shadows

You can adapt this ritual for any tool or object. Before you begin the ritual, take a moment to compose a short book blessing that you will copy into the book itself during the ritual.

What You Need:

- Piece of plain white cloth (of natural fibers)
- Book, tool, or object to be dedicated
- Small bowl of salt or soil to represent element of earth
- Stick or herbal incense to represent element of air
- Censer or heatproof dish (and charcoal tablet if using herbal incense)
- Candle and holder to represent element of fire
- Small bowl of water to represent element of water
- A prepared book blessing
- Anointing oil (plain olive oil, or a blend of oils for blessing)

What to Do:

1. Center and ground. Create sacred space or cast your circle, as you wish. Either is appropriate for this ritual.
2. Invite elemental energy to be present. For example: *I call you, powers of earth, / To be present as I dedicate my book of shadows. / Welcome to my circle.*
3. Perform Step 1 for all four elements.
4. Invite the Divine to be present in the form of the Goddess and God. Use the names of specific god-forms if you work regularly with them.
5. Pick up the white cloth and run it over the book's covers, both inside and out. Run it gently along the edges of the pages. If there are any tags or foreign matter on the book, remove them. In this step you are physically cleansing the book.
6. Take a pinch from the bowl of salt or earth and sprinkle it on the book, saying: *Book, I purify you with the element of earth. / May your energy be purified of negative energy. / So mote it be.* (If you wish, you may purify with the remaining three elements, although the salt will suffice.)
7. Center and ground again. Hold the book in your hands and open your energy center. Allow your awareness to flow into the book. Feel your energy filling it, and visualize it glowing brighter and brighter. As the glow of your energy permeates it, visualize any other energies clinging to it simply dissolving away. Say: *I consecrate you, book of shadows / to serve as my record of my magical work. / I charge you by all that I hold good and true: / Be for me a faithful record of my life, my work, and my love. / So mote it be.*

8. Take the book and touch it with another bit of salt or earth; pass it through the smoke of the incense; let the light cast by the flame of the candle dance across it; and sprinkle it with a few drops of water. As you do so, imagine the energies of each element filling the book with positive energy and the touch of elemental energy that will further consecrate it.

9. Open the book and write your book blessing inside on the first page. Take a touch of oil on your finger and draw whatever symbols of protection and wisdom you desire, if any, on the front and back covers. As you do, charge the book with the positive energy that you and the elements have created.

10. When you are done, thank and release the deities you have invited to be present. Thank and release the elements for their help as well. Dismantle your circle or declare your ritual complete if you have used sacred space. A simple "It is done" can suffice.

Some Final Thoughts on Simple Rituals

Now that you understand the differences between these simple rituals, you can go about creating your own versions. Your own words and actions will have more meaning than anything you find in a book or get from someone else. Creating your own set of both simple and complex rituals will help consolidate your practice of Wicca and help develop your beliefs. You can research symbols and color correspondences to add certain energies to your rites, and further tailor them to your needs and desires.

Chapter Six

Enriching Ritual

In this chapter you will revisit your basic Wiccan tools and learn new ways to use them. You will also explore more advanced tools and practices, such as sacred drama and the uses and influences of masks, ritual garb, and symbols to bring new depth to your spiritual practice.

Basic Tools Redux

You most likely already have at least five of the basic tools: the knife or athame, the cup, the wand, the pentacle, and the book of shadows. Wiccans often forget that the altar is also a basic tool, although you may not have a permanent altar; many Wiccans use whatever space is available to them at the time and consecrate it as required.

Do you really *need* these basic tools? Absolutely not. If you believe that you do need them to practice Wicca, then you may have limited yourself to a very material practice. Tools are *symbols* of archetypal energy, and no more than that. We will touch upon the basic tools briefly, then explore the altar and book of shadows in more depth.

The Athame

The majority of Wiccan beginner books teach that the *athame* is a tool used only to direct energy, never to cut anything physical. However, many Wiccans who follow more practical paths influenced by kitchen witchcraft or hearthcraft use their athames for any magical purpose, be it cutting ritual cakes, carving symbols into candles, cutting thread used to sew magical pouches, and so on. Other Wiccans may prefer to have a dull athame (ensuring that it will never cut), a single-edged athame (symbolizing the dual purpose of practical use and spiritual use), or a double-edged athame (symbolizing the double-edged responsibility to the self and to others when handling power). If a Wiccan wishes to keep the athame as a tool that directs and cuts energy alone, then sometimes a second, white-handled knife is used for the more mundane tasks; this is called a bolline, and may have a curved or sickle-shaped blade.

Some Wiccans don't like using a knife at all; they feel that it is an aggressive weapon with no place in the loving practice of Wicca. Others use it exclusively for casting their circle or for lowering it into the cup during the symbolic Great Rite, preferring to use their hands or a wand for other rites requiring an athame.

If you have never used your athame for anything other than raising it in salute to the four quarters, challenge yourself to use it in place of your wand when directing energy. Vary your practice and note how the experience affects your ritual.

Make sure your athame is clean at all times. If you use a tarnished athame with a blade that has bits of candle wax on it, what kind of effect does that have upon the energy you are channeling through it? (Experiment and make notes. It may not matter to you, though it might shock someone who identifies as a very traditional Wiccan.)

Wiccans tend to prefer using a *wand* or an athame, but not both equally; whatever works best for you is the right choice. Some prefer the wand because it is less aggressive.

If you use an athame or a wand regularly, try performing a ritual with only your hands instead. What sort of differences do you sense?

The Staff/Spear

If you already use a wand, try making a *staff*. A staff is similar to a wand or athame in that it directs energy. You can research the various energies associated with different trees to select a wood that will resonate well with your own personal energy. A staff measures approximately shoulder height. You can buy a dowel of the wood of your choice and cut it to the correct size, or carefully prune an appropriate branch from your chosen tree with respect and permission from both the tree itself and the owner of the land it grows on. If you are using a fresh branch, strip the bark from it, unless you wish to keep it on, and carve bits of it away as your design. Allow a fresh branch to dry out thoroughly before you personalize it. You can carve, paint, and decorate it to your taste with leather, crystals, feathers, or other meaningful symbols.

You can also further customize your staff to become a spear. Create the basic staff, and then carefully make a vertical cut in the upper end. Insert a small metal blade blank, spearhead, or crystal into the cut, then firmly wrap it with a length of leather cord and tie it off securely. A drop or two of glue before you wrap it can help secure the spear point. The spear can function as a combination of athame and wand.

The Cup

The *cup* is variously used to hold the physical representation of water on the altar, as a receptacle or an offering, or as a vessel to share communion. A thrifty Wiccan or someone who has limited space can use it for all three. You can pour out the water you bless as a representation of elemental energy as an offering to trees or plants outdoors or give it to your houseplants; you may even drink the water you bless. Taking it into your body during the ritual is a wonderful way to absorb the qualities of the element of water. (Do this only if you haven't added anything to it during the blessing process, and only if whatever tool you may have touched to it during the consecration or blessing is clean.)

The Pentacle

The *pentacle* comes from the ceremonial magic elements used by Gerald Gardner to initially bulk up Wicca. The pentacle is a flat disk of wood, earthenware, or metal, inscribed with the five-pointed star known as the pentagram. The points of the star may reach the edges of the disk or may stop about an inch from the edge, and an engraved circle may surround the star. The pentacle represents the element of earth on your Wiccan altar, although some use it to represent Spirit. It's not only symbolic, however. It can be used to ground objects or to charge them. You can serve the food part of your communion on it. While the pentagram is a common symbol on the pentacle, you can experiment with other symbols, such as triskeles, ankhs, Celtic knots, and other meaningful symbols that inform your practice and personal spirituality.

The Altar

The altar is your basic workspace. It's not necessarily a permanent fixture, especially in the case of a Wiccan who lives with others of non-Wiccan spirituality, or one who lives in limited space. However, as time goes by you can take even the most basic altar further.

The altar is placed according to the cardinal direction to which your practice is tuned. Lots of books will tell you to place it in the east area of your circle, the direction associated with intellect and knowledge. Other books will tell you to orient it toward the north, the direction associated with manifestation and power. Some Wiccans are horrified by the idea of moving the altar if they've become used to working with it in the east. However, it's not heresy to shift your altar according to the ritual you're performing. You have the luxury and freedom of being able to place the altar wherever you please. If you feel a particularly strong connection with the element of water, why not experiment with orienting your altar toward the west? If the deity you work with is primarily associated with fire, try placing your altar in the south area of your circle.

Try positioning your altar in different directions around the circle according to the seasonal shifts. At Yule place it in the north. At the vernal equinox place it facing toward the east, the direction associated with new light and new beginnings. At Midsummer orient it toward the south, the direction of fire, power, and energy. At the autumn equinox orient it toward the west, the direction of farewell and harvest.

Wherever you aim your altar, make sure you leave enough room to move around it. An ideal position for the altar is right in the center of the circle, which allows you great freedom of movement to access it from any angle.

If you are lucky enough to have a permanent altar, you may have to leave it where it is and build your circles around it. A permanent altar can literally store energy for you. Rather than grounding excess energy into the earth or into your tools at the end of a ritual, ground it into the altar. As a focus for worship, your altar builds in energy as you practice; using this method of grounding means that your altar eventually develops into a tool with power of its own that you can tap into.

The way you set out your tools upon the altar is up to you; there is no rule dictating where things must be. Most Wiccans, be they eclectic or traditional, have some sort of representation of the four elements set up somewhere on their altar. These can be physical representations, such as salt for earth, water for water, a candle for fire, and incense to represent air. Or the representations can be symbolic, such as an athame for fire, a wand for air, a pentacle for earth, and a cup for water. Representations can be a blend of physical and symbolic. Know, too, that your elemental representations can serve multiple purposes: the salt and water can be combined to create a consecrating liquid, or the incense can also be used as an offering to the deities with whom you work.

Some traditions switch the elemental correspondence for the athame and wand, choosing to align the knife with air and the wand with fire. Use what works best for you!

Arranging these items on your altar, along with candles to provide illumination, statues or deity representations, other tools you require in your ritual, and often food and drink, can be a challenge. If you like to have your book of shadows on hand when you do a ritual, you need room for it on the altar as well, which can make things even more crowded. Just know that you're free to move things around as you require, and that certain objects can serve double duty. Try shifting the position of your tools as you progress in your studies; you may be surprised to find a new combination that further enhances the energy flow in your altar.

Consider a Secondary Altar

If your altar is becoming too crowded, consider making a secondary altar in the circle on a small side table or box, and orient that toward the direction you wish to work with in the ritual. Setting up a secondary altar can relieve space issues on your main altar, particularly if you use a permanent altar that has a lot of ongoing work set up on it. You can have a main workstation and a secondary one without losing focus, as long as you consecrate the secondary altar as well. Do the opening and closing ritual framework at your main altar, and your main celebration or work at your secondary altar. When you're finished, touch both the main altar and the secondary altar at the same time to make a connection. Siphon off the energy from the secondary altar and allow it to flow through you into the main altar. No energy is lost, and in the future you can draw energy from the main altar and transfer it to the secondary altar in the consecration process, if you like.

Minimalist Altar Setups

Whether you work with a permanent altar or a temporary one, you don't need a full altar setup every time you do ritual. Experiment with using the fewest tools possible to strengthen your ability and skill at handling energy and visualizing during ritual. Try doing ritual with nothing but a bowl or cup of water and a small dish of salt. Use your hands in place of all other tools.

If your altar is temporary, select an altar cloth or a stone to serve as the heart of your altar. This cloth or stone will be the link to your altar—you can place excess energy into the cloth or stone rather than into whatever you are using as your temporary workspace. An altar cloth or stone is portable, so you can carry it with you to wherever you need to set up your workspace.

Also, consider creating a shrine to a deity you work with on a regular basis, or simply to the Lord and Lady. A shrine is a place to honor and to leave offerings, and a physical point of spiritual contact where you can connect to a deity. An altar can be used for these things as well, but a shrine is not a workspace like an altar. Shrines are easier to set up and maintain because they aren't as noticeable. A shrine can consist of a postcard, a specially charged crystal, a plant, or a small statue. Using a shrine as a focus for these activities can also help clear up your main altar area.

The Book of Shadows

There are few records left by people who practiced the Craft before the twentieth century. Our idealized vision of the perfect book of shadows—a large, hand-bound book full of notes, diagrams, and secrets—probably did not exist among folk practitioners through the ages, as these people were likely illiterate and paper was in short supply for a large part of the past two millennia.

A popular term for the idealized book of shadows is a *grimoire*, which is French for "grammar." This is an appropriate connection, because grammar explains the basic structure of a language and your book of shadows explains the structure of your spiritual path and evolution. But the most accurate definition of a grimoire is in fact an established collection of spells used as a workbook, such as *The Key of Solomon the King* and *The Book of the Sacred Magic of Abramelin the Mage*. A traditional grimoire does not contain the full set of information necessary to perform the rituals and spells inside. Additionally, a grimoire tends to be associated with ceremonial magic, as opposed to the more organic practice of spiritual paths such as Wicca.

When you began recording your journey along the Wiccan path, your book of shadows probably had many other people's rituals and poetry and such in it. If you work with a group, you may be given an existing set of rituals or lore used by your group to add to your book of shadows. As you progress, the book of shadows evolves into a more personal record of your own experiences. It becomes a place to write down research, your own poetry, sketches, spells and rituals you write, dreams, meditations, and various musings. For the advancing Wiccan the book of shadows becomes, in essence, a spiritual journal and archive, and possibly your most valuable tool.

Your book of shadows is your most reliable resource for looking over earlier work and evaluating progress, evolution, and development. This is part of why it is vitally important for you to keep detailed and up-to-date records. Consistent use of your spiritual journal helps you organize all the bits of interesting information you discover on your path. It also provides a concrete record of your work, so that you can understand where you might have gone wrong in spellcraft or ritual, or re-create successful rituals and spells. Overall, a well-maintained book of shadows helps you keep your practice consistent.

There is, of course, no single, ultimate book of shadows that is more valid than any other. Each is relevant to its respective user. Each coven has its own master book of shadows that collects a body of rituals and lore unique to that coven or tradition, used regularly, that reflects their spiritual expression; each practitioner—whether a solitary Wiccan or a member of a coven—also has their own. A spiritual journal is a private record and collection, not a universal one; it is a reflection of your soul. This is why collecting only the work of others in your book leaves your practice one-dimensional. Messy though they may be, your dreams, hopes, flights of fancy, and attempts at spellcraft and ritual design are vital aspects of your spiritual development.

There exist two main approaches to the spiritual journal. The first approach treats the book of shadows as a polished final copy of all your work. Spells and rituals are copied into it only after they have been thoroughly perfected through experience.

The second approach treats the tool like a complete collection of all the spiritual work you do. It includes records and texts of rituals and spells, clearly annotated notes taken from books you've read, recipes for herbal concoctions you've tried and notes on the results, notes on meditations and dreams, divination records, correspondences, and so forth.

For many, a book of shadows is more valuable when it encompasses the entire spectrum of the spiritual journey. If you note down only what works, you lose the benefit of being able to look back on your mistakes (one of the best ways to track your progress). It's nice to have a beautiful, formal version of your book of shadows, but a spiritual journal is much more helpful in learning and growing if it contains records of your progress and thoughts as well.

It can be difficult for a spiritual person to accept that they weren't as advanced a few years ago, or even a few months ago. Yet denying one's past self is not a healthy thing to do. A Wiccan understands and accepts the former self with love. Embracing your older records and book of shadows is one way to accept that, once upon a time, you were just a beginner and didn't know as much as you know now. Wiccans are eternal seekers. Even after years of experience we humbly acknowledge that there is always more to learn, and still deeper levels of our own souls to plumb. The saying "The more I know, the less I understand" is entirely true for anyone practicing Wicca.

Organization

Is your current spiritual journal a disorganized mishmash of information? Consider numbering the pages and creating an index to fasten into the back. When this book fills up and you begin a new book, consider dividing the new book into sections marked by sticky tabs, and separating the information you put into it by subject or category. Alternatively, you can buy separate books for separate things—such as one book for correspondences, symbols, lore, and ritual-related information; a second book for notes, working out spells, and recording experiences from casting spells; and a third book for meditations, dreams, and divinations. You could also choose to keep an herbal grimoire with samples and pressings of herbs, sketches, and both medicinal and magical correspondences.

To Type or to Write?

In these modern times it's often more practical to keep information in an electronic format. Many modern Wiccans possess a spiritual journal in two formats. They type and store some of the work on a computer and write out the rest. Perhaps you've heard others insist that you must keep your book "in your own hand" and this has made you feel conflicted about keeping a computerized version of your spells and rituals.

There are several advantages to maintaining your book of shadows on a computer:

- Your material will be easy to find.
- It will be easy to read.
- It is easy to run off a copy of the text for use in ritual without having to handle your entire spiritual journal.

- You can keep a backup copy somewhere else, such as a safe-deposit box, in case of disaster.

There are also drawbacks to having your spiritual journal on your computer:

- A computer file is cold and has less personality or character than a handwritten book.
- You run the risk of accidentally erasing the file or having it corrupted.
- A virus or hardware failure can destroy your entire machine if you are not properly protected.
- At times it can be inconvenient to print out the necessary pages.

The advantages to writing out your book of shadows by hand are numerous. Writing things out by hand is an excellent method through which to memorize material. A handwritten book of shadows possesses charm and character, and can be much more conducive to creating an atmosphere appropriate to ritual. It's also deeply personal. Drawbacks include that handwriting can be hard to read by candlelight or moonlight, and if for some reason you lose your book, you've lost everything.

Ultimately, your spiritual journal is exactly what you make it. It is a blend of your choices, your personal style, and your practice. Many Wiccans use a combination of the computer and handwritten forms. Any spiritual record files on your computer should be backed up and stored in another location, just in case. You can choose to type up the text of a ritual or any information you've researched, print it out, and put it into your physical book of shadows for ease of reference, where it will provide a nice contrast to handwritten information.

The Art of Spiritual Record-Keeping

Now that you understand how important it is to be able to trace your evolution, you might have to adjust or update the way you keep records. Take a look at how you have been recording your rituals, spells, and dreams. Are they clear? Do your notes immediately raise the memory of the ritual in your mind? If you had to redo this ritual, could you perform it again from your notes? Have you recorded both the short-term and long-term results?

To ensure that you are recording all the details, you can prepare a record sheet in advance of performing a planned ritual or spell. Then you can use the sheet as a checklist while you're gathering supplies or when you're setting up.

How to Record a Ritual

This is a basic list of the information that should be included in the record of any ritual you perform:

- **Name of ritual and type of ritual.** This should be at the top of the sheet.
- **Date and time that the ritual takes place.** If it's an original ritual, you may also add the date and time you composed it.
- **Moon phase.** Add the moon sign if you know it, as well as other pertinent astrological information.
- **Weather.** This is more important than you think.
- **Location of the ritual.** Is the ritual in the living room, backyard, etc.?

- **Your health.** If you are female, also note where you are in your menstrual cycle.
- **Purpose of the ritual.** This may be obvious from the name of the ritual. For example, "Imbolc Ritual" is pretty self-evident, but a ritual named "Prosperity Ritual" might require a little more information, such as the circumstances requiring such a ritual to be performed.
- **A complete list of the tools and ingredients required.** This is vital for future reference and reuse.
- **Deities invoked.** This is only necessary if you work with more than one established pair.
- **The entire text of the spell or ritual.** If you use a standard circle-cast and set of quarter-calls, then you can simply indicate this. If you wrote new ones for the occasion, include the full text.

All this can be prepared before the ritual, and you can work from the record itself if necessary. After you are finished, note down this extra information:

- **Approximately how long it took to complete the ritual.**
- **Your immediate reaction to the ritual.** How did the ritual work out and how did it feel?

Leave room for the following information, to be added at a later date:

- **Short-term results.** What do you notice over weeks following the ritual?
- **Long-term results.** What sort of changes have you observed over the following months or years?

How to Record a Divination

Recording divinations can be tricky. Some people believe that the entire layout of cards or tiles should be recorded, while others think that just noting down your general impression of each divination is adequate. The answer lies somewhere between the two extremes.

If you are doing a series of divinations for people, you may not have the time to write out all the information in detail. In that case, note down the most striking pieces of information that you uncover. If you are reading for others, too, they may be uncomfortable with you writing down details while they are there.

Here is the sort of information that diviners find useful to consult in retrospect:

- The date and time
- Moon phase (and sign if you know it), and any other pertinent astrological information
- The location of the reading
- The weather
- Your health
- Name of querent (Who has come to you for this reading?)
- System of divination used (if a tarot deck, identify which one)
- Layout or spread used
- Symbols in key positions (What cards, runes, or patterns emerged as important?)
- Your interpretation of the spread (What is your overall evaluation of the answer to the querent's question?)
- Details you wish to remember
- Feedback (this allows you to note down any response you receive from the querent, both at the time of the reading and at a later date)

If you are doing divination for yourself, then you can be as detailed as you like. You can sketch out the entire spread and indicate what symbols appeared in which positions.

Other Ritual Elements

A ritual is more than words on paper, and it incorporates more than the basic Wiccan tool set. In a theatrical presentation visual elements such as makeup, costume, props, lighting, and sets influence both the performer and the spectator. The use of these elements in a ritual can equally amplify certain moods, energies, and qualities, even when you are the only one present. The following sections will explore these elements as techniques you can use to deepen your ritual experience.

Costume in Ritual

Costume is worn for many reasons. In a crowd it is worn to distinguish the performers or ritual leaders from the audience or participants. Costume can be dramatically spectacular, thereby heightening the sense of expectation and excitement. Costume is also a very clear way to identify whom a particular performer represents. Costuming appeals to the inner child in all of us who loved to play dress-up. And wearing appropriate costumes allows us to communicate through the use of color, symbol, and archetype. Costume can also reinforce the theme of a ritual, or support the cultural connections a ritual might have.

You may already have a special outfit that you wear only for spiritual work, and this is a tremendous aid in getting into the right headspace for ritual. For special rituals, you may wish to create a new ritual costume to deepen or highlight your experience. As tempting as it may be to try to re-create the authentic vestments of a Babylonian temple priestess, my advice to you (which comes from years of costume experience in theater and ritual) is three-fold:

- **Think simple.** You can always dress it up or down with accessories and props.
- **Think practical.** Is a four-foot headdress really going to enhance your ritual, or just make you move awkwardly?
- **Think versatile.** A basic costume element that can be reused in another ritual is a better investment.

If you practice alone, you may consider costume in ritual useless because you are your own audience. There might be no other people present to witness your costume, but there are a host of other reasons to enhance your ritual with costume. Costume is a visual element, but it also possesses certain associations for the person wearing it. How often do you dress the part when you are going out to a particular venue? Our outward appearance can reflect our inner mood, and it can influence our emotional and mental state as well.

Following are some more ritual costume tips. The advice may sound like common sense, but you would be surprised by how many people ignore common sense when designing and constructing ritual garb.

1. **You need to be able to see out of your costume.** Not being able to see your full workspace is a very frustrating limitation in ritual. You need your complete field of vision to react to potential hazards (and face it, you've got them—brooms, staves, large cauldrons, fires, pets wandering through the space, candles, or elemental representations at the quarters). A complex and detailed mask may look and feel dramatic, as may a veil or a deep cloak hood over your face, but if you can't see clearly, you're asking for trouble.

2. **You need to be able to move in your costume.** Tripping as you move is one of the easiest ways to snap yourself out of the correct mindset for your ritual. The costume may look beautiful when you stand still and look in the mirror, but think about where you want to perform your ritual, as well as how much you need your balance and complete use of your limbs. Skirts or robes that drape on the floor are beautiful, but they're impractical if you plan on moving around in your ritual, especially outside. Flowing sleeves and loose hair are among the most common fire hazards in ritual. Gloves can be slippery and hot. Make sure that you can use your hands, walk normally (if not climb over rocks outdoors), and sit down comfortably. Additionally, your costume needs to be able to fit in your chosen ritual space. A towering crown, large feathers, or a wide collar may look ideal in a design, but they can easily catch on doorways or tree branches.

3. **Your costume needs to be comfortable.** When you construct your costume, try to use cottons, silk, or at least blends with a high percentage of natural fibers. These allow air to pass through them, as opposed to plastics and polyesters that retain heat and

can become quite uncomfortable. Manmade fibers can also be more difficult to care for. Masks must be light, have adequate ventilation, and rest comfortably on your head or face, without irritating tender areas such as eyes or ears. It's very common to remove a mask at the end of a ritual and discover the inside slick with perspiration. If you really wish to use a particular mask that creates this sort of problem, wear it only within the ritual. Make donning a mask part of the ritual itself, if you like. If you want to use your mask but cannot wear it in ritual, consider setting it at the center of your altar or hanging it above the altar so that you can see it, and use makeup instead.

Props in Ritual

In theater and other forms of performing arts a prop (short for *property*) is anything that a performer carries while on stage. Theoretically, your basic Wiccan tool set constitutes a form of prop. There are plenty of other ritual aids that can serve as props, though. For example, you may wish to create a scroll from which to read an important invocation or oath in a formal ritual. At some point you may wish to make a small representation of a tree for a specific ritual, or a Brigid's Cross for Imbolc. If you work with Egyptian symbolism, you may wish to construct and use a sistrum or ankh in your rituals. Props can be used regularly, or they might be one-time-only things constructed for a special ritual.

Lighting in Ritual

You probably already play around with different types of lighting. Many Wiccans love to do ritual by candlelight, because it evokes a more relaxed and intimate atmosphere. Glaring electric light has less romance to it. Of paramount importance is having enough light by which to read and move about safely during your ritual. If the idea of lower light appeals to you but you cannot use candles, consider using a simple dimmer switch on your electric light, easily installed.

Sound in Ritual

If you've never done ritual to music, you're missing a whole dimension! By choosing music carefully, you can enhance a ritual beyond its basic effects.

In general, music without words is the best accompaniment to ritual. In terms of accompaniment, the music must never distract from the theme of the ritual, nor should it interfere with the energy you are weaving. Words tend to distract our conscious mind as we try to catch what's being said. Experiment with the orchestral score to a film that has a similar feel to the ritual you will conduct.

When using music, you can choose a single musical cue to perform a symbolic central action. For an important ritual you may choose to program a whole series of musical cues, one after the other, to help time each step and to reinforce the type of energy you will be working with in each of those steps.

When working with music, it can be best to have the audio equipment nearby with a remote handy, and a written-out playlist with the pertinent track listings attached to the text of your ritual. If you work alone, consider creating a playlist of your favorite ritual music and using a speaker.

Some purists believe that electronics interfere with the energy you raise. To each, their own. The only way to find out how you feel is to experiment.

The Element of Drama in Religion

Now that you've explored some of the theatrical techniques you can incorporate into your rituals, the next step is to infuse your rituals with drama. Worship is inherently dramatic, with its rituals and usage of symbols supplying an agency by which we encounter and develop a deeper understanding of faith.

Most religions have some form of dramatized stories central to them. The benefits are two-fold: a worshiper understands the story on a personal level, and together as a unit the performers and audience explore the meaning of the story to the community as a whole.

Drama has always held close association with religion. Think about the ritual enactment of the success of the hunt in pre-Christian societies. Hunters symbolically acted out through dance and movement the chase and subsequent capture of their prey in order to ensure success in the real hunt. This type of ritual drama was a form of sympathetic magic. In ancient Greece the worship of Dionysus included a festival wherein his story was acted out through dance and ritual theater. During the Middle Ages Christian churches dramatized the stories of the life of Jesus, using storytelling as an alternate teaching method for those who could not read or write. Even the basic modern Christmas pageant that reenacts the story of Christ's birth is a form of ritual drama. At Succoth many Jewish families reenact the time the Israelites lived in tents in the wilderness by building and spending time in small lean-tos or shelters.

Drama in a ritual context allows you to gain new insights and see things from a different point of view. It can also be a lot of fun, as it's an advanced form of "let's pretend" that rests on the strength of your belief and your commitment to a goal.

Role-playing is one of the methods humanity has developed to allow us to explore new viewpoints by acting them out. Role-playing in a religious context can be particularly effective. The emphasis is not as much on depicting a character to an audience; instead, the activity explores the mindset or personality of the role you have chosen to take on. Role-playing is also easy in that it requires no script—it can rest entirely on the ritualist improvising on the spot.

Sacred Drama

Role-playing in a ritual setting does not require complex verse or choreography. In fact, miming emotion can often be a powerful method of immersing yourself in a myth or sacred drama. How does Demeter feel when her daughter Persephone is taken away from her? By imagining yourself in her situation and immersing yourself in her grief, you can gain a new insight into the turning of the seasons through autumn and winter.

Movement and improvised dance are also easy ways to work through a myth. In a group situation one or two people narrate a story while others mime it. The descent of the Goddess is a popular story enacted in this way, as is the battle of the Holly King and the Oak King.

If you're a solo practitioner, you can record yourself reading the story aloud, and play it back during ritual while you act it out. Limit yourself to exploring one character at a time. If you try to do all of the characters in the story at once, you will end up exhausting yourself. Furthermore, each figure in a myth or sacred story has a different lesson to teach you—pursuing them all at once can result in muddled messages.

By dramatizing myth or sacred story, you can make discoveries about your spirit and your connection to the themes of the myth. How well you can act is unimportant. This exercise is more about your experience and your emotions as you take part in the story.

Read Chapter Twelve to learn about aspecting a deity, a practice sometimes associated with ritual drama.

If you are limited in your range of movement because of disability or space constraints, the use of puppets is an excellent alternative. It also allows you to design and craft the puppets, which can then become cherished ritual tools in their own right.

Something to keep in mind when you experiment with sacred drama is to keep it short and focused. If a myth has several sequences, perform one sequence at a time, allowing time for the lessons and experiences to sink in. Long, drawn-out ritual dramatic exercises can quickly lose cohesion and obscure the lessons encoded in them.

Chapter Seven

Crafting Rituals

In this chapter the various stages of a Wiccan ritual are separated and explained. You will learn the basics of how to craft your own rituals.

The Importance of Ritual

Performing ritual serves to mark important occasions and offers an opportunity to celebrate. Regardless of religion and cultural setting, societies automatically create rituals to mark graduations, marriages, deaths, birthdays, and anniversaries of every sort.

A ritualized setting provides a time and place for us to interact with our subconscious, the collective unconscious, and the astral plane, and commune with the gods and the universe via symbols, tools, and energy. In a way, ritual provides a distraction for the conscious mind, giving it something to do while our subconscious does the work for change.

Wiccans perform ritual to give energy to the earth and to the gods, to receive energy in return, and to keep the energy moving in an ongoing dialogue between the earth, the Wiccan, and the deities. Through ritual we connect to the ceaselessly cycling energy that powers life itself. In a religious context Wiccans use ritual to celebrate, to honor, and to create an atmosphere through which our minds will be more receptive to whatever programming we wish to give them.

I recommend that you write a standard ritual framework for yourself that can be adapted with the change of only a few words for any ritual setting or purpose. A framework comprises sacred space/circle, elemental call, and deity invocations, and then the reverse at the end. You'll be doing yourself a huge favor with such a structure by freeing yourself to focus on the central actions and themes of your ritual.

Different Levels of Ritual

Ritual does not mean that you have to perform a large, elaborate sequence of actions every time. There are several different degrees of ritual.

- A **spontaneous ritual** is an off-the-cuff ritual with only a basic outlined plan of action. This kind of ritual is easy for a solo practitioner to perform, because there's only one person involved. In groups a spontaneous ritual can be performed as long as every participant knows the purpose of the ritual and everyone works together toward that, but it can be hard to control in large numbers. Certain types of purposes are ideally suited to spontaneous ritual, such as folk magic, which often calls on the practitioner's intuition to perform whatever may be required at the time.
- **Relaxed rituals** may be scripted, or they may include only some scripted material, such as a regular circle-cast or quarter-calls. A full set of tools is not necessary, and in fact the only tools that may be involved are the ones you yourself choose to involve. If you use a script, a relaxed ritual allows you to freely deviate from it if inspiration strikes you. The common steps may be combined rather than individually delineated; for example, you may create sacred space and invoke the quarters simultaneously. The framework may be outlined, but the central working of the ritual may be spontaneous or only have a vague outline.
- A **formal ritual** is usually the kind performed for very important occasions. A full script is prepared, and no deviation from it is allowed. Each step reaffirms the point of the ritual and is clearly delineated and set apart. A formal ritual usually includes the detailed use of specific tools and involves most if not all of the common steps, all clearly set apart.

Common Components of Ritual

The basic ritual format is remarkably flexible. It can expand to include extra steps or collapse to encompass only a minimum of action.

While not every ritual will demonstrate the following steps, they are frequently used and familiar to most Wiccans as a part of practice:

- Preparing for ritual
- Creating sacred space
- Casting a circle
- Calling the quarters
- Invoking divinity
- Performing the Great Rite
- Working magic and/or recognizing the celebratory reason for the ritual
- Raising energy
- Observing communion
- Thanking divinity
- Releasing quarters
- Opening circle
- Grounding and centering

The following sections will explore these steps. The steps are grouped into three sections to illustrate how they function within the ritual sequence.

Ritual Opening

The ritual opening comprises all the steps leading up to your actual working or celebration, whether it is an esbat, a sabbat, or a spell.

The opening covers the creation of the temple and the invocation of the elements and deity to consecrate the space.

Cleanse

Before you begin your ritual (unless it's a spontaneous ritual), there are several preparatory steps to cover. You will want to design and plan your ritual, which includes collecting any tools or supplies you have decided to use.

1. **Prepare your space.** Rearrange the furniture if necessary, physically tidy up, and dust and sweep the area. Lay out your tools, and set up the essentials on your altar.

2. **Prepare your body.** Take a cleansing bath or shower to wash away physical dirt and relax your body, ridding it of stress and tension. (If this isn't possible or practical, use an alternate method, such as wafting incense smoke around your body or dabbing salt water on your forehead, heart, solar plexus, abdomen, and hands and feet.)

3. **Prepare your mind.** Spend a few minutes in meditation to relax and focus your mind as well. Center and ground, and make sure that you're in the right frame of mind for ritual. If you can't bring your mind to focus, then either cancel the ritual and reschedule it or do a less formal ritual instead, such as an honoring or balancing ritual.

The purpose of these preparatory steps is to get you into an altered state and a ritual frame of mind. You need to be relaxed but alert, focused but abstracted, and open as well. Once you're in the right frame of mind, you're ready to begin. It is important to realize that *this is the process in which ritual actually begins.* The ritual isn't launched with your words—it begins with your frame of mind. Some Wiccans might even argue that preparing the self qualifies as part of the ritual, for it serves as the first step in attaining that frame of mind.

Purify

As you physically cleansed yourself, cleanse the energy of your ritual area as well. (There are a variety of ways to do this, as explored in Chapters Two and Five.) This is done as a sign of respect: you're about to create a sacred space in which you will perform a religious ceremony. Cleansing the space both physically and psychically also eliminates any stray bits of negative energy (or other energy) that could distract you or run counter to the purpose of your ritual. You are creating a clean slate upon which to work.

If you feel it is necessary, you can purify any tool you intend to use in the upcoming ritual, even if you have cleansed, consecrated, and blessed it on a previous date. This doesn't have to be a full purification, merely a quick and gentle touch to reaffirm your connection with the tool. If you are reusing something such as a stone that you intend to program or enchant during the ritual, you will definitely want to purify it to create a clean slate upon which your purpose will imprint.

Sacred Space and Your Circle

Some Wiccans like to create sacred space before they cast their circles. Others feel that the physical and psychic cleansings create enough of a foundation upon which to cast a circle, and cast the circle at the step where you would consecrate to create sacred space. Some Wiccans feel that the casting of a circle drives back any unsupportive energy, and thus replaces the need for cleansing and purifying before it goes up. However, going through the cleansing and purifying process allows you to prepare your mind as well as the space. They're important steps to include before any ritual, whether you intend to perform that ritual in sacred space or a circle.

When you cast your circle or consecrate the space, include in the words you use the reason why you're having the ritual in order to reinforce your intent. For example, if you are casting a circle for a ritual to honor the Goddess, you might use a phrase such as "Be for me a place between the world of mankind and the realm of the gods as I create this temple in which to honor the Lady this day" or "...as I create this space in order to work this healing ritual."

Call the Quarters

At its most basic, calling the quarters means inviting the elemental energies associated with each quarter to be present for your ritual. Depending on how you phrase it, you may be asking them to bless the circle, lend their energies to your ritual, or protect your space. Ideally, you should use a similar form for all four calls to maintain consistency, both for ease of remembering and to keep the energy levels within the ritual as even as possible.

Calling all four quarters creates a certain balance, but you do not have to call all four at every ritual. There may be a time when you wish to employ a very specific kind of elemental energy in your ritual, and you may choose to open only the quarter associated with that energy. Experiment with this technique, and keep notes on your success.

A *quarter* is a catchall term for a symbol and all the related associations. If you call on the element itself at one quarter, maintain that thematic consistency and call on the appropriate element in all four quarters. Don't call on the element in one, a guardian in another, and a watchtower in the next quarter. Quarters are more than just elements or directions. They're the cardinal directions with elemental and symbolic correspondences built up over the ages.

Think about why we call them quarters. The standard Wiccan ritual space is a circular shape. A quarter of that shape is a wedge that covers a full quarter of that space. When you call a quarter, you're not calling a single point. You're summoning elemental energy to flow into a full quarter of your circle. Imagine the energy flowing toward you in a gentle wave, and know that the entire quarter is keyed to that energy. As in raising the circle, adding a line about the purpose of the ritual helps key the elemental energy to your objective. Something basic will suffice, such as:

Element of Water, bless me with your presence in my circle as I honor the Lady this day.

It's vital to have clear in your mind what you are doing at each quarter. You need to understand the actual energies you are stirring with the familiar words. Many people recite something along the lines of:

Hail, guardians of the watchtowers of the [direction], lords of the powers of [element]! I summon, stir, and conjure thee to witness this rite and to guard this circle.

If you deconstruct the call and look at each part of it, you'll see that you're doing something more complex than simply "calling the quarters." Summoning, stirring, and conjuring forth are very different processes. Think about them, look up the definition of each word, make notes, and make a conscious choice to use a word associated with whatever you're invoking.

Some calls muddle the concepts entirely, and summon "the guardian of the watchtower" at each quarter no matter what the ritual is designed to accomplish. This is a general misunderstanding and a misapplication of the two concepts.

- A *watchtower* is derived from ceremonial traditional practice and indicates a watching presence that witnesses your ritual. Each watchtower is associated with a cardinal direction but is not directly associated with the corresponding elemental energy. For example, the watchtower of the north is not equivalent to the energy of the earth.
- A *guardian* is exactly what the word suggests: a protector. A guardian is an intermediary between you and the outer worlds. If you do call a guardian, its attention will be focused *away* from your ritual, not upon it. A guardian cannot be a witness, nor can it bless or lend its energy to your work. Again, a guardian is not directly associated with the energies of the element usually assigned to the quarter.

Invoking Deity

As a Wiccan, you worship the God and Goddess in some form or another, according to your personal belief system.

When you invoke a deity, you open a channel between the energy of that deity and your ritual space. More often than not, the presence of the deities is felt through a sensation of peace or relaxation, an awareness, or a simple intuition that the deity is now in attendance. The energy begins to flow into your temple space, and you can then incorporate it into the energy of your space. Some Wiccans allow the energy to simply wash over them and fill their circle, while others consciously drink it in and absorb it themselves, or channel it into a receptacle such as a statue or a symbol for the duration of the ritual.

It is important to remember that you are not *holding* the gods there by having invoked them and their energy. You are not commanding with your invocation; rather, you are inviting the energy of the deity or deities to enter your space. Including the purpose of your ritual in your invocation further fine-tunes the energy that you are weaving, keying the energy to the objective as you build the opening of the ritual.

Courtesy and tradition dictate that you invite in the God first, leaving the Goddess to make her grand entrance alone with all eyes upon her. According to your personal choice, you may invite the Goddess and God separately, or together as a pair. To invite them together, for example, you can say:

> *Lady of peace, Lord of light,*
> *I call to you this day*
> *From this place not a place, and this time not a time.*
> *I invite you to join me within my temple,*
> *To bless this ritual of healing with your presence.*
> *Welcome, bright Lady; welcome, forest Lord.*
> *So mote it be.*

Invoking the gods as a pair is a great way to maintain the idea of balance flowing through your ritual. There may be times, however, when you wish to invoke only the God or the Goddess, to focus specifically on working with one type of energy or one individual god-form. In that case, you have a choice. You can invoke the generic form of both deities, and then proceed to invoke the presence of the specific deity with whom you wish to work, or you can invoke only one deity.

The Central Working

Often the previous steps associated with the opening of the ritual are part of a Wiccan's regular practice, the text and actions being the same for each ritual, as are their mirror images performed at the end of the ritual to formally close it. What changes from ritual to ritual is what you do between the opening and closing.

When teaching ritual design, we can use the metaphor of a sandwich to explain the structure of a ritual. The two slices of bread are the customary opening and closing procedures. The filling of your ritual sandwich is what changes every time, and it is the set of practices that differentiates an esbat from a sabbat or a prosperity ritual.

The central portion of your ritual begins with a statement of purpose: why are you here? Not only does this serve as an official beginning, but it also signifies that the creation of your temple is complete.

The Great Rite

The Great Rite is an essential part of the Wiccan mythos, although it appears in other religions as well. The Great Rite invokes what is possibly the greatest magic of all: the union of the Goddess and God. This is far more than a mere physical joining. It is a complete merging of energy and identity, forming a joyous and awe-inspiring balance— the Union of the Whole. The Great Rite celebrates fertility, life, and unity, and is the ultimate rebalancing of a situation that requires the harmony of the associated energies to be drastically restored.

The Great Rite has two forms. The *Great Rite in truth* involves the physical, spiritual, and energy union of a male and a female within a ritual situation. Usually the representatives of the Goddess and God are a high priestess and high priest. This is most often used within a traditional Wiccan environment. It is different from the *symbolic Great Rite*, which is performed using a ritual tool associated with female receptive energy, such as a cup or cauldron, and a ritual tool associated with male projective energy, such as an athame or a wand. In a ceremonial fashion the male tool is lowered into the female tool, and the act is performed with awareness and intent.

The symbolic Great Rite is often performed directly after the invocation of deity, symbolizing the balance of deity energy now present within the ritual space. A form of it is sometimes used to bless the cakes and wine before communion, the athame being lowered into the chalice of liquid to represent the fertility of the God energizing the contents, and the pentacle's feminine energy energizing the cakes upon it.

Working Magic or Recognizing the Celebratory Reason for the Ritual

The focal ritual action may be celebration, as in a sabbat or a rite of passage; worship, as in an esbat; or the raising and releasing of energy toward a goal, as in a spell-centered ritual. Different steps are associated with each sort of ritual. If you're doing a spell, then you decide what it includes, and how to approach it. Refer to Chapter Four for information on spells, Chapter Eight for information on sabbats and esbats, and Chapter Nine for information on rites of passage.

Raising Energy

Depending on the purpose of a ritual, the step of raising energy is performed in different ways. If you are casting a spell within the religious context, then you will raise energy to be released toward the goal of the spell. If you are honoring deity, then you may raise energy to share with that deity. If you are celebrating a sabbat, you will raise energy to share with the earth and aid it in its work, and in thanks for what the earth provides us. In a group the ritual leader will collect and guide the energy as it is raised by the coven, releasing it at an appropriate moment. Solitary Wiccans will be in control of this step on their own.

There are a variety of ways to raise energy in spiritual practice. Some will be more appropriate to your ritual than others. Methods include:

- Meditation, visualization, and concentration
- Chants and invocations
- Incense, oils, and potions
- Dancing and drumming
- Offerings

(For a more in-depth look at these methods and others, you can refer to my book *Power Spellcraft for Life*.)

Grounding after raising and channeling energy is an important step. Reestablish your connection with the earth and release any excess energy, or draw energy up to replenish your own if you released too much. Refer back to Chapter Four to refresh your memory about grounding and working with energy.

Observing Communion

Eating and drinking is another way to reestablish your grounding, although it should never completely replace grounding with the earth. Taking in food and drink helps adjust blood sugar levels, and engages you in a purely physical action to give you a moment to think and come back to yourself. This rite is often referred to in traditional Wicca as *cakes and ale* or *cakes and wine*, although commonly the food is bread and the drink is water or juice.

An offering to the gods of both food and drink signifies that we acknowledge where the sustenance came from and that we will always share.

Often in this step you will ask for the blessing of the gods upon the beverage and the food. This reinforces the fact that this step is not just a simple restocking of energy but a method by which the energy and blessing of the gods are shared with the ritualist.

This step exists for another reason as well, a more symbolic one. The wine is sometimes blessed by enacting the symbolic Great Rite, if the Great Rite has not been performed after the ritual opening to honor the balance of male and female energy. Here's a sample cakes and wine rite:

Cakes and Wine Rite

Use this rite as a basis for constructing your own rite of communion for use in your rituals. Remember to purify both the beverage and food before using them. You do not need large amounts of food and drink; this act is symbolic.

What You Need:

- A cup or chalice
- Beverage of choice (can be in the cup before ritual or in a separate container)
- Food of choice (can be placed on your pentacle or waiting on a separate plate)
- A small empty bowl for an offering

What to Do:

1. If the food and beverage are not in the cup and on the pentacle already, place them there before beginning this rite.
2. Center and ground. Hold up the chalice reverently. Imagine that you are presenting it to the Goddess herself. Say: *Bright Lady, bless this drink with your love and grace. / Imbue it with your blessings, that I may drink it to honor you, / And in so doing share in your wisdom, knowledge, and love. / So mote it be.*
3. Allow yourself to sense the grace of the Goddess filling the cup. Place it on the altar.

4. Hold your hands over the food on the pentacle or plate. Say: *Mighty Lord, bless this food with your strength and love. / Charge it with your blessings, that I may eat of it to honor you, / And in so doing share in your wisdom, knowledge, and love. / So mote it be.*
5. Visualize the power of the God flowing into the food.
6. Break off a piece of the food and place it within the small offering bowl. Pour a few drops of the beverage over it, saying: *Food of the gods, I return you to the gods. / Lord and Lady, I thank you for your manifold gifts and blessings.*
7. Eat a few bites of the food and drink a sip of the beverage. As you take the food and drink into your body, open yourself to absorbing the mingled energies of the Goddess and God. This is a wonderful time to meditate, or simply commune with the gods and feel their love and support.
8. Leave the offering bowl on the altar. When your ritual is complete, you may leave it there overnight, or place it outdoors.

Closing the Ritual

The steps in closing the ritual mirror the steps performed as the ritual was opened—the same steps, only in reverse.

Thanking and Releasing Divinity

As you have begun your ritual with structure, so too should you close it with structure. Often we focus on preparing for and building up to the symbolic central work of the ritual to the point that we forget that there must be equally secure closure to the ritual as well. This is important both for balance and for a correct dispersal and grounding of the energies with which you have worked.

The first item in the sequence of closure is the thanks given to the deities whom you have invited to be present for your ritual. This is your opportunity to express your gratitude and communicate your feelings of honor for being able to work with them and to share in their energy.

Often performed simultaneously with giving thanks is offering farewell to the deities. This is the moment when you release the divine energy you have invoked. Some Wiccans call this action "releasing the gods" or "dismissing the gods." Because you have not forced the presence of the deities, "releasing" them does not mean you are opening a cage to allow the deities their freedom, and "dismissing" them does not imply that you are demonstrating authority over them. To bid the deities farewell, to dismiss them, or to release them is to inform them that the ritual has ended.

There are other reasons why this step is important. It may sound ideal to have the energy of the gods stay with you even after the ritual, and you may be tempted not to formally thank and release them. This is not a good idea. As you formally invited them, you should formally bid them farewell. Having that sort of energy about without a circle to focus and contain it can create a very unpredictable situation. Additionally, it is impolite and inconsiderate to forget to alert your most important guests that the ritual is over.

You may dismiss the God and Goddess separately or in the same speech. If you invited them as a pair, bid them farewell as a pair; if you invoked each separately, each should be thanked and released separately. A general thanks and farewell to both the Goddess and God can be similar to this:

> *Lady of peace, Lord of light,*
> *I thank you for your presence within my temple this day,*
> *And for lending your power to this ritual of healing.*
> *I honor you, my Lord and Lady,*
> *And bid you farewell.*
> *So mote it be.*

If the deities were invoked separately, then as a sign of respect the Goddess is often thanked and released first, as she was the last into the circle.

Releasing Quarters

Release the quarters in the same way you invoked them. If you called upon guardians, release those guardians; if you invoked elements, release those elements; if you called for witnesses, release those witnesses from their task. Release the quarters in reverse order—the last in is the first out.

If you don't release the quarters after a ritual, the elemental energy will remain with you, and this will be intensely unbalancing. It's less dangerous than having a specific god-energy haunting you or your space, but it can be incredibly disorienting nonetheless. Dealing with a surfeit of elemental energy in your life is not worth the trouble. Take the time to dismiss the quarters properly.

Opening the Circle

The step of dismantling the circle is also known as dissolving the circle, releasing the circle, or opening the circle. Theoretically, a circle is weakened and destroyed if you breach its borders. However, this is an unwise way to dissolve it after a ritual. Your ritual has been coded for a certain purpose all along, and you've been careful and precise throughout. Why toss it all away by not tidying up?

If you have cast the circle in one direction, release it in the opposite direction. Remember, Wicca is about balance. Formally declaring the circle terminated aloud helps send a psychological signal to your subconscious that it can begin to emerge from the ritual frame of mind it's been working in.

Grounding and Centering

Take a moment to assess how you feel after your ritual. Whether you're humming with excess energy or weak and shaky, sit or lie down on the ground and allow your own energy to equalize with that of the earth. If you have excess energy, allow it to seep away; if you're low on energy, absorb some from the earth.

Acting In Accord

We sometimes forget that while the formal ritual may be over, the energy we have raised and released is still moving. A bonus post-ritual step can serve to reinforce the energy's action. Wiccan author Amber K calls this "acting in accord." By acting in the physical world to strengthen the opportunity for manifestation or further harmony, you increase the ritual's potential yield of success. For example, if you have done a ritual to improve your health, follow it up with a visit to your doctor and discuss ways in which you can improve your diet, exercise regimen, and lifestyle (if applicable). Rituals and spells cannot solve the problem on their own; you must pair them with action taken beyond your ritual space.

This step also helps remind us that Wicca is an everyday spirituality practiced in our everyday lives.

Building a Ritual

You've just explored each step and its importance in the ritual. Once you've reached or reconnected with an understanding of the basics, you are set to construct your own rituals. You will find that there are three distinct levels to the creation of a ritual.

First Level of Ritual Construction

You begin constructing a ritual by defining the purpose of it. Brainstorm about the central theme of your ritual and write down on a piece of paper or in your book of shadows your ideas regarding the theme. Once your ideas are recorded, take them and work to further refine them down to a single sentence.

Next, you must define who your audience is. If you are a solitary Wiccan, you are your own audience. If you are part of a coven and doing a ritual with others, you will need to consider how many people there will be and what their needs are. For now, though, concentrate on what you're looking for in this ritual.

Once you know what the central theme of ritual is and what your spiritual needs are, you can schedule the time of the ritual and choose a place in which to perform it. You can be as vague as you like (a Friday) or as specific as you like (moon phase, season, specific date). Make sure that the physical location you choose will be available at that time.

With all this information determined, you can decide what type of ritual to perform—simple, relaxed, or formal.

Second Level of Ritual Construction

Once you have the basic needs outlined, you can begin to refine things a bit more. Does the theme you've chosen suggest a particular cultural connection that you can explore as you write your ritual? Do you have an established pantheon of gods with whom you work, or will you research deities and find one that suits your purpose? Perhaps the purpose of the ritual directly connects to a cultural practice or deity already, such as an Imbolc ritual being traditionally connected to the pan-Celtic goddess Brigid.

Think about correspondences. What tools and symbols will amplify and support the purpose of your ritual? Research the herbs, stones, colors, and symbols that are sympathetic to your purpose. Think, too, about the elements and cardinal directions. Perhaps you might choose to invoke only one or two elements that are strongly associated with your ritual theme. You might choose to orient your altar toward one of the elements connected to your ritual purpose.

Third Level of Ritual Construction

Take time to think carefully about a single focal event for the ritual that will serve as the central axis of honoring or energy raising. The focal event must be sympathetic to the theme of the ritual to make it as cohesive as possible.

For example, in an Earth Day ritual I once led, the focal action consisted of the participants mixing small individual bowls of earth in one large cauldron, and then running their hands through it, pouring positive energy into the soil, which was later divided evenly among them to take home and add to their gardens. Other examples of focal actions include the passing of a flame from one candle to another through the darkness at Yule, and the creation of small sachets of herbs to throw into a bonfire or cauldron fire at Midsummer.

Decide now whether or not you will use your established framework of sacred space creation, quarter-calls, invocation of divinity, and so forth, or if you wish to write new ones to reflect the ritual. If you do choose to create a new ritual framework, allow yourself plenty of time for rewrites and to familiarize yourself with the new text. Memorizing your invocations will allow you to focus on handling the energy as opposed to reading from a piece of paper.

Once you have your ritual framework and central activity written out, put away the ritual before you look at it again. After a few days or a week has passed, reread the ritual aloud to ensure that it flows smoothly. Walk through it in the space you intend to use to ensure that the flow of physical movement is smooth as well.

How long your ritual will be depends on you and your participants. You know by now how long you can stay focused on what you're doing; how long a group can focus depends on the individuals making up that group. Time your walk-through of the ritual; if it seems too long, revise it and cut out extraneous parts, or combine steps to make it more focused.

Look over your ritual to make sure that you have a balance of intellectual, emotional, and physical work to involve the various parts of your brain. If the bulk of your ritual entails sitting and thinking, your mind can easily wander and this will weaken your focus. If your entire ritual consists of dancing and chanting, you might not be allowing your subconscious enough time to absorb the purpose of the ritual.

Focusing on and planning for a ritual will *not* detract from it. Preparing for a ritual thoughtfully, thoroughly, and responsibly over time reinforces the intent of your ritual and begins coalescing the energy associated with it before the ritual even starts. This preparation doesn't remove energy from later steps; it only reinforces the energy.

Performing Your Ritual

When the day for your ritual arrives, build in plenty of setup and takedown time. Go back and look at the list of common steps, and estimate how much time you'll need to adequately prepare yourself both physically and mentally before your ritual actually begins.

Sabotaging Ritual

We have all had our share of rituals that just didn't happen as we wanted them to happen. Usually we have no clear idea why they failed, and we're left asking ourselves what went wrong. Here are some possible reasons:

- **You were unprepared.** If you're not in the right frame of mind, then you're not going to be able to make the transition into ritual mode. You won't be able to relax enough to channel the energy required to make the ritual successful. You should be in ritual mode, relaxed but alert, calm but ready to act at a moment's notice. Ideally, this state includes being centered and grounded. If you have problems with this stage, reread Chapter Four and practice the exercises within it. Making sure that you're centered and correctly grounded will eliminate many of your problems.

- **Your emotional state was inappropriate.** There's something important implied in the idea of being relaxed and focused: you can't be in an agitated emotional state and expect to perform a ritual. If you're highly upset, don't waste your personal energy on performing a ritual. You won't even be able to connect clearly with the energy around you, which means that you won't be able to handle that energy either. Emotion does drive a successful ritual. The trick is to balance strong emotion with careful control.

- **You were in poor health.** When you're ill, your personal energies are out of balance. This means that your ability to handle other energies will be affected as well. Working ritual when you are ill can make you even sicker, leaving you drained and your personal resources dangerously low at a time when your body needs them. Remember, it takes energy to raise energy, and when you're sick you usually don't have a lot of energy to spare. If you're performing a ritual to improve your health and to increase your own vital energy, then ill health is not necessarily an obstacle. However, it's important to ensure that the ritual you perform isn't too stressful, and to use a gentler method of raising energy than you might usually employ.

- **You aimed too high.** A common flaw in many rituals is too much complexity. If your ritual is florid and calls for you to light six candles at once, chances are that you'll be focusing so hard on what you're reading or physically doing that you won't be able to mesh correctly with the Divine, nor will you be able to handle the energies you raise. The pretty bits of ritual are supposed to give your subconscious mind symbols and colors to inspire it, not to confuse it with lots of words and actions. This is not necessarily the case for talented writers, for whom writing a detailed ritual may be an act of worship. Nor is this true for talented actors, who use florid passages to open themselves up to the energy of the Divine. For the rest of us, though, an overly detailed ritual step can impede the very purpose of the ritual itself.

• **You used unfamiliar ritual structures.** If you create a new ritual framework every time you perform a ritual, you're not allowing yourself to become familiar with a regular ritual structure. By using an established ritual structure, you become comfortable with the words and requirements of each step. This frees you to focus more on the handling and skillful manipulation of energy.

• **You second-guessed yourself.** It can be difficult to stop second-guessing your abilities and experiences. If you're working alone without someone else to help you reaffirm your actions and intentions, you may feel confused by your results. If you're working with a group, the feedback you get about your participants' experiences may be confusing or even contradictory. Let go and trust in your intuition and in the love of the gods.

When Not to Do Ritual

Theoretically, ritual is always appropriate, as long as you are in a mental and physical state to carry it out properly. Ritual must have a purpose in order to have meaning, however. Simply running through a ritual will not provide you with the harmony you seek.

There are times when meditation is more appropriate to achieve a goal such as rebalancing your energy.

The act of going through a familiar ritual can have a soothing effect on your psyche and soul, but to do this without connecting to the true purpose of the ritual is to deprive yourself of the true experience. Performing a ritual for solace instead of the ritual's actual purpose is taking advantage of the ritual.

If you find yourself wanting to do ritual for the sake of doing ritual, then ask yourself why. It can be easy to become addicted to the feeling you associate with a ritual; feeling energized, relaxed, or high is a common result. To perform a ritual is a means to an end, not an end in itself.

If you find this happening to you, choose a simple honoring ritual that allows you to connect with a deity and work on the problem with the deity. Afterward, create a ritual that you can perform if the situation arises again—perhaps one centered on exploring the inner self, or a ritual that gives you a formal space in which to meditate. Chapter Ten addresses meditation as a part of ritual work, as well as other subjects such as prayer and invocations.

Chapter Eight

Sabbats and Esbats

This chapter will help you reexamine your perceptions of the sabbats and esbats. Added to your knowledge of the steps for designing a ritual, this information can help you create more meaningful rituals for yourself and others.

What Are Sabbats and Esbats?

Sabbats and esbats form the basic natural cyclic structure upon which the Wiccan practice is founded. By performing rituals to commemorate various points in these cycles, you can communicate with the cycles as they progress, and with the associated energy as it shifts and transforms. To achieve this communication, there are different practices associated with each type of sabbat and esbat ritual.

One of the major traditional differences between these two is that esbats are a time to worship and do magical work, and sabbats are a time to celebrate and honor the earth. Sometimes Wiccans choose to differentiate in another fashion, with esbats as rituals for the Goddess and sabbats as rituals for the God. This association can become clumsy and unnecessarily exclusionary, however, because it emphasizes a division where none exists. The God and Goddess are seen as two halves of a whole, and to celebrate only one half of a glorious unit seems self-defeating. It is the interplay of masculine and feminine energy that propels each cycle forward; removing one of those energies cripples the cycle.

Keeping Sabbat and Esbat Work Separate

Lots of Wiccans allow magical work to creep into their sabbat rituals. Be careful with this. Sabbats are good for ritual drama and meditation upon the turning of the seasons, and attuning to the energy of the earth as it cycles through its phases. An esbat is usually reserved for magical work. Spellcasting, scrying, divination, and other related practices come into use during esbats.

An attunement can be done through a symbolic action to reflect the sabbat theme or the season. The line between that symbolic action and magical work blurs if the symbolic action becomes too complex. Think about older sabbat-related symbolic actions. For example, northern European people used to roll a burning wheel down a steep hill after sunset on Midsummer's Day. The action reflected in miniature what was going on in the season: the bright, fiery sun had passed its zenith and was beginning to decline, and the days would grow shorter from that point onward. A sabbat is a time to interact with the energy of the changing season.

Confusion can arise from the combination of the idea of a symbolic action and the concept of a spell. A spell has a specific intent in response to a specific need. Components are gathered to lend supportive energy to obtain a goal. The components are activated together with energy raised by the spellcaster, and then released toward the goal. A symbolic action, on the other hand, is performed in sympathy with a greater event. Energy may be raised through the symbolic action, but it is to contribute to the cycle as it shifts, or to enhance the attunement the Wiccan has with the macrocosm. The performance of a sabbat ritual leaves the Wiccan energized and attuned, in harmony with the greater scheme of things. No spell needs to be cast to achieve a goal, for the goal is what the ritual itself already provides. Esbats are where we work for ourselves; in a sabbat ritual we work for nature and for the Divine.

Sabbats

On a basic level sabbat rituals celebrate the turning of the Wheel of the Year. Western society usually points to the Judeo-Christian use of the term *Sabbath* as the likely source of the term Wiccans use to describe their holy days. But the Judeo-Christian word has earlier roots in the Greek word *sabatu*, meaning "to rest."

Sabbats are solar-based and agriculture- and earth-oriented. Most sabbat practices derive from social interactions within an agricultural community, and carrying them out can be challenging to modern Wiccans who live in urban setting. However, the sabbats offer you a completely different perspective on the seasonal cycle— one that can be remarkably deep and rewarding. Celebrating a sabbat helps you connect directly with the seasonal energy and forge a very personal relationship with it. You are not constrained by anyone's idea of what makes a "proper" sabbat ritual. In fact, as an eclectic Wiccan, you have the right and the responsibility to connect with the seasonal energy in your own location to exact the maximum benefit from the celebration. If it's usually snowing heavily in your location on the vernal equinox, connect with that energy instead of performing a sabbat celebration honoring the first signs of vegetation as British-based Wicca does.

It's important to remember that Wiccan rituals are *inspired* by older practices, and that they are not direct, honest, unchanged re-creations. We know very little about our pre-Christian ancestors and how they worshiped. It is safe to posit that the modern Wheel of the Year as expressed through the eight sabbats was unknown to our spiritual ancestors, no matter what culture they came from (although some of the traditions may have been similar and practiced in a secular form). Research on the sources of the names for the eight sabbats reveals a multicultural influence, further reinforcing the notion that no single culture ever celebrated these precise eight festivals as we celebrate them now.

Once societies turned from hunting and gathering to a more sedentary, agriculturally based way of life, the ancients likely broke down their year according to their climate and the practices associated with their agricultural cycle.

The ancient Irish, for example, recognized two seasons: winter (*Geimhreadh* in the old Irish) was the fallow season, and summer (*Samhraidh*) was the growing season. Neo-Pagans sometimes refer to this split as the light half of the year and the dark half of the year. The light half encompasses May through October, and the dark half encompasses November through April. Keen Wiccans will note that these halves turn on two very important sabbats: Beltaine, the festival honoring life and fertility; and Samhain, the festival honoring death and darkness. Other Wiccans prefer to place the turning points of the light and dark halves of the year at Midsummer and Midwinter (the two extremes of light and dark) or at the equinoxes (the points of balance between light and dark). The philosophy is similar—the division simply rests on a different method of dividing the seasons.

> The sabbats mainly honor the Goddess in her aspect of mother earth and the God in his forms of solar king and vegetation god. The interaction between the two provides the energy required to advance the cycle of the agricultural year.

There is an important concept associated with spiritual practice that tends to be overlooked when it comes to examining basic elements of Wiccan practice, such as sabbats. That concept is *evolution*. Slavish adherence to the basic associations of each sabbat listed in beginner books misses the point. It is important to allow your personal connection to the sabbat to influence how you commemorate it, both in everyday life and within a ritual context.

One of the keys to developing and deepening your practice of Wicca lies in a dynamic recognition of and interaction with the natural cycles. Harmony not only means that your personal energy matches that of the cycles of the world around you; it also means that your own personal energy has been enriched in some way. This is most effectively accomplished when that dynamic interaction between the cycles takes place. Observing is one method of learning; internalizing and then applying your new insight in a practical fashion further develops that knowledge into wisdom.

Additionally, seek inspiration in the culture of the pantheon you work with. To take other festivals and simply plug them into the places on the modern Wheel of the Year can diminish both systems. But there is no reason why you cannot honor additional holy days, or thoughtfully employ themes sacred to another culture in addition to those associated with the modern Wheel of the Year. Incorporating old folk traditions into the ritual expressions of modern Wicca is a wonderful way to honor the past, as long as you remember that what you are doing is a modern *interpretation* of something that *may* have happened in a similar fashion once upon a time. As long as the tradition makes sense to you in your perception of the sabbat, and functions consistently with the rest of your seasonal perceptions (both within that sabbat and the overall sabbat cycle), there is no reason for you not to include a cultural tradition in your sabbat celebration. The possibility that the ancients did not celebrate the equinoxes has no bearing on how valid they may or may not be today. Use your discretion, and do what feels right to you.

Common Rites Found in Sabbat Rituals

Of the common steps listed in Chapter Seven, there are certain steps that usually appear in a sabbat ritual. The idea of incorporating cakes and wine is important because the sabbats are based on an agricultural cycle, and at each sabbat a different agricultural event is marked. The cakes and wine rite offers you the opportunity to give thanks for that agricultural event. The feast following the sabbat celebration often reflects the newly available foods from fields or herds. Both events celebrate that availability once again and offer to the gods the first servings of the seasonal food or drink. Additionally, each sabbat has certain actions that celebrate the achievements or the theme associated with the season.

The Order of the Sabbats

The fascinating thing about a cycle is that it has no beginning and no end; the sequence is an ongoing round that never ceases. Humans tend to pin down birth as the beginning of a cycle and death as the end, though in the natural order of things death is the opportunity for another birth of a different kind. Some Wiccans consider Samhain the end of the cycle, as it correlates to a death of sorts, and Yule as the first sabbat of the cycle, as it corresponds to birth. For this reason, Samhain is often referred to as the Wiccan, Witches', or Celtic New Year. Remember that the ancient Celts believed the day ended with sundown, so every night was the beginning of the following day. (This is the reason why some sources indicate that certain sabbat days begin the evening before the commonly used date.)

Other Wiccans prefer to consider Imbolc the beginning of the cycle because it is traditionally associated with the beginning of spring—a time of birth and new beginnings—and it is the first sabbat to appear in the calendar year.

It is most accurate to view the Wheel as a cycle, with each sabbat having its place, and no true beginning or end, only the ever-cycling shift of the seasons. If you set up these sabbats on a pie chart, you'll see that each sabbat has an opposite partner directly across from it. Interestingly enough, each of these partners encapsulates a complementary energy or festival. We'll take a look at these partnerships as we explore the sabbats.

Quarter and Cross-Quarter Days

The greater sabbats, known as the quarter days, are Imbolc, Beltaine, Lughnassadh, and Samhain. The remaining four sabbats are referred to as lesser sabbats, or cross-quarter days. We know these as our solstices and equinoxes, astronomically calculated by the moment when the sun crosses into the zone of a specific constellation in the sky.

The division between quarters and cross-quarters is not random, although it may seem that way at first. In fact, the quarter days derive from the old English rent-paying days, when tenants of farms were required to give their landlords a portion of their crops or herds in exchange for the right to use the land. Celebrating the day on which one pays rent may seem counterintuitive, but it made sense in a social context. People had to travel and gather in selected places to complete the rent transaction. Where there was a gathering of people who didn't see each other frequently, markets and fairs were created, stimulating general community and family bonding.

While the quarter days have gravitated to set dates on the calendar, they are technically calculated by the progress of the sun. When the sun reaches a point measuring 15 degrees into the astrological sign active at the time, the astronomical date of the quarter day occurs.

Try the following experiments:

- Celebrate Imbolc when the sun reaches 15 degrees of Aquarius.
- Celebrate Beltaine when the sun reaches 15 degrees of Taurus.
- Celebrate Lughnassadh when the sun reaches 15 degrees of Leo.
- Celebrate Samhain when the sun reaches 15 degrees of Scorpio.

Evaluate the difference both in the natural energies around you and in your own energies as you perform the ritual. You may well discover that the astronomical date of the sabbat better reflects the flow of the year's energy and your personal energy than the calendar date does.

The cross-quarter days, which fall halfway between successive quarter days, were added to the calendar much more recently. While the ancients built massive earth mounds and stone circles to mark the precise moment of one or both solstices, there is no proof that they commemorated the equinoxes in either structure or ritual. In fact, Ronald Hutton, in his book *The Stations of the Sun*, assigns the importance of the equinoxes to the influence of American culture:

During the twentieth century the notional beginning of spring came itself to be moved backwards to the vernal equinox, by a slow process induced by the mass media. This was part of an adoption of the American system of reckoning seasons from the solstices and equinoxes, which works admirably in the climate of most of the USA, but is nonsensical in the rhythm of the British year. (Hutton, p. 145)

Likewise, many residents of North America are puzzled by the traditional British association of spring with the sabbat of Imbolc, for the climates rarely match up. Think of the Wheel of the Year as a metaphor for the life cycle, whether it is reflected in your geographical locale or not.

Following is a sabbat-by-sabbat exploration of the themes and symbolic actions that you can incorporate into your sabbat celebrations.

Yule
December 20–23: when the sun passes into the sign of Capricorn

The word *Yule* comes from the Norse *jól*, which was a feast with merrymaking to honor the gods and to encourage plenty and peace. This term likely traveled to the British Isles with the Saxons and became attached to what would become the twelve-day Christmas season. The *jóls* took place more than once a year, often around Midwinter and again around Midsummer, but the name persisted only with the native winter festival.

Also referred to as Midwinter (because it falls halfway between Samhain and Beltaine), Yule occurs on the astronomical date of the winter solstice, which means the date varies from year to year. Most calendars will note the precise time of the winter solstice and of the other three seasonal dates. Many cultures associate the winter solstice with the rebirth of the sun and the return of the light after the days have grown shorter and the nights longer. From approximately this point onward, the sun will wax larger and brighter once again until Midsummer. Yule celebrates the joyful promise of new growth in the darkness of winter.

The Wiccan mythos situates the Goddess's birthing of the new God at this time of the year. The Wiccan mythos also gives us the legend of the Oak King and the Holly King battling at each solstice to determine who will rule as the vegetation god. The Oak King wins the battle at Yule and takes his place as the king of waxing light, deposing his brother, the Holly King. Some Wiccans view this ritual battle as a ritual sacrifice of the deposed Holly King, who gives himself to the earth so that it may prosper through his decay. Others perceive it to represent the battle between the returning sun and the entrenched darkness, and perform acts of sympathetic magic such as the lighting of candles and fires

Items such as candles, fires, and evergreen in the form of boughs and trees are typical Yule symbols. The flames symbolize the sun, while the greenery represents life everlasting, despite the apparent death of the earth. The Yule log unites these two symbols.

to encourage the sun's strength so that it will win and force the darkness back for a time.

Many traditions associated with this festival have carried over into other cultural celebrations. In the agriculturally based societies of the past, winter meant a time of hardship for many if crops were poor or the herds thin in the time leading up to it. Hospitality and generosity were valued at this time of year, when cold and hunger were all too common. Through the ages specialty foods (including sweets) were developed to celebrate the milestone of surviving to see the light return. Feasts are also prepared to honor the deities associated with the season.

Yule is an opportune time to introspect on the darker parts of your life. The longest night provides plenty of time to meditate on the darkness in your soul, and how your soul is affected by the fading light. After such a meditation think about what the returning light will give you, and what the growing light will reveal as the darkness begins to shrink. Midwinter takes place in the fallow time of year, when the earth seems dead—but deep inside the darkness a seed is being nourished, held in warmth and love, awaiting the light of the sun to awaken it and coax it into life once again. Every sabbat is a wonderful opportunity to think about the cycle of life, but Yule in particular offers an opportunity for hope for renewed life, health, and light.

Celebrating Yule

Yule is a remarkably easy sabbat to celebrate, because, as with the other sabbats, many of the symbolic actions spill over into secular celebrations of associated holidays. One of the traditional events associated with the Yule sabbat is the feast. You can cover this by engaging in the typical seasonal gathering of family or close friends to share food and conviviality. Your spiritual reasons for the celebration do not have to be shared by the others at the table—you are all celebrating joy at a time of friendship and warmth.

The Yule log is a central symbol in the Wiccan Yule ritual. Depending on the sources you consult, the Yule log is most often a piece of oak decorated with evergreen boughs, mistletoe, and holly. The log symbolizes the balance of the God (the oak) and the Goddess (the evergreen), and is placed in front of or atop the altar.

In the past the Yule log was burned as an act of sympathetic magic to encourage the sun to return. If you have a fireplace, you can witness the glorious and moving transformation of the log as it burns and releases the energy with which you have charged it. Older traditions call for retaining a small charred piece of the log, preserving it all year to help start the fire in which the next year's Yule log will burn. The ashes of the Yule log are said to have great power. Keep them and sprinkle them in your garden in the spring to bless the garden.

In these modern times, when not many people have access to a working fireplace, the Yule log is often treated as a candleholder. By drilling one to three holes in the top, you can place candles in the Yule log and burn those instead. The number of candles you use will depend on what you want the log to symbolize:

- One candle, often red or yellow, represents the God as he is born.
- Two candles, often green and red, represent the Goddess and God.
- Three candles, often white, red, and black, can represent the Triple Goddess or the triple aspects of both deities.

Wreaths of evergreen, ivy, holly, and mistletoe are also commonly used in Wiccan Yule rituals. Some Wiccans lean these items against the altar, or place them on the altar's surface. You can place the wreaths around a red taper or pillar candle that represents the God. The circular shape of the wreath recalls the cycle of the seasons and the cycle of life. Once the wreath has been blessed by its inclusion in the ritual, hang it on your door, in your window, or wherever it may extend its blessings to the rest of your property or personal space.

A vigil by candlelight on the longest night of the year is another common modern Yule tradition. Ideally, you can light the candle in the center of your wreath or the candle(s) in your Yule log at sunset, and they burn all night, their warmth and light coaxing the sun to return. At dawn the flames are extinguished. If you have the opportunity to burn your Yule log, this makes a wonderful beginning to the Yule vigil. Don't worry if the log is not big enough to burn all night. The Yule log only needs to be the first log on the fire; it will "feed" the subsequent logs you use, extending its magical association to the fire itself as long as it burns.

As romantic as this tradition sounds, it is a challenging one to actually perform. Many of us are expected to work the next day, and it's impossible to forgo a night of sleep. If you are celebrating alone, it can be more challenging than staying awake in a group of people—it's too easy to fall asleep, no matter how spiritual you feel. However, you have the freedom to perform your Yule ritual at whatever time you choose, or break it into two parts. Perform part of your Yule ritual at sunset the evening before the day the solstice arrives: Bid farewell to the sun as it vanishes into the darkness for the longest night, extinguishing your candle to symbolize the darkness of the longest night. Then, wake up before dawn (or earlier than that if you usually arise before dawn in late December) to light the candle once again and perform the second half of the ritual to welcome the sun's appearance.

If you choose to burn a candle all night while you sit through your waking vigil, take the proper precautions in case you do nod off:

- Burn a candle that will last for at least sixteen hours.
- Have a fire extinguisher as well as water and/or sand nearby.
- Burn the candle in an appropriate holder that will catch any spilling wax.
- Don't place the burning candle in a draft.
- Make sure there's nothing too close that might catch fire.
- Move decorations or greenery away from the candle, or spray greenery with plenty of water to wet it before you light the candle, if it cannot be moved.
- If you choose to decorate your log or God candle with artificial greenery, place it a safe distance away before you light the candles; artificial greenery burns quickly and more dangerously than real evergreen does.
- Try using jar candles—the tall, pillar-type candles encased in glass that burn for forty hours—for safety. Jar candles are stable and reliable, and the flame is kept away from flammable substances and protected from drafts.
- And finally, LED candles might not have the romance of a real flickering flame but may be your safest choice.

Imbolc

February 1–2, or when the sun reaches 15 degrees of Aquarius

Imbolc, one of two sabbats associated directly with a specific deity, is a festival to celebrate the beginning of spring. Imbolc's partner across the Wheel is Lughnassadh, the Feast of Lugh.

The modern eclectic Wiccan perception of Imbolc comes from three very different festivals. Imbolc is one of the clearly Celtic festivals, with no Saxon influence. The Celtic Imbolc is celebrated from sundown on February 1 to sundown on February 2. This agricultural festival marks the lambing and calving season in the British Isles. Candlemas, which is the Catholic festival of the purification of the Virgin and the blessing of candles, is celebrated on February 2. From these two festivals comes the modern Wiccan Imbolc feast of purification and growing light. The third important festival that has influenced Imbolc is *Lá Fhéile Bhríd*, or Brigid's Feast Day, and this influence is perhaps the most popular for modern Wiccans. Celebrated in Ireland and the outer isles of Britain and Scotland, this festival honors the goddess (and later saint) Brigid. Her name is spelled and pronounced in different ways depending on the location in which she was worshiped. The original translation of her name in Irish Gaelic meant "bright flame," and from this translation the association of Brigid with fire arose.

Brigid is one of the original triple goddesses—not the maiden-mother-crone triptych postulated by Robert Graves in the mid-twentieth century, but the triple-sister form that predates the modern conception of the age-separated Triple Goddess.

Brigid is quite a multipurpose goddess, encapsulating different associations from different cultural and regional affiliations, such as healing, poetry and the arts, and smithing. Over time her association with poetry and inspirations has led her to be a goddess often invoked for creative purposes. She is generally assumed to be a gentle goddess, but one of her cognates, Brigantia, was the martial goddess of a warrior tribe in the British Isles, and any deity associated with smithing has a connection to warcraft (as well as hearthwork).

In some myths Brigid is the maiden goddess who seizes control of winter from the Callieach, the crone goddess of winter. In the climate of the British Isles and in western Europe the beginning of February does indeed bring the first real signs of spring. In the British climate farmers plough and prepare the fields for crops. Cattle and sheep feed on the newly sprung grass, and give birth to young, which results in the production of enriched milk. The new lambs and calves are signs of new life, confirmation of the ongoing life cycle. Brigid is associated with cattle, sheep, and milk; in fact, some of the later saint depictions show her with a churn or pails of milk. For these reasons milk forms a focal point in many Imbolc rituals.

In the modern Wiccan mythos the infant God born at Yule is now a child, nicely fitting into the Brigid and Imbolc associations of children and hearth and home. Imbolc is one of the sabbats that revolve around fire, as both a source of warmth and a source of purification. By this point the returning light has noticeably lengthened the days.

Celebrating Imbolc

Key to the concept of Imbolc are the first stirrings of the potential for life after a period of seeming lifelessness. As the weather varies so drastically among where Wiccans now live, focusing on the return of spring during Imbolc can have less meaning than the concept of purification in your ritual. On the other hand, depending on your locale, perhaps the promise of coming spring is a welcome concept after you've been frozen in snow and ice for a few months!

A symbolic action derived from the old Irish Imbolc traditions is to leave a ribbon or a square of cloth outdoors overnight, where it is said that Brigid will bless it as she passes on her feast night. This cloth or ribbon can then be used to aid you in healing spells and rituals during the year.

The purification of the dullness that can come with darkness is one of the popular images found in eclectic Wiccan practice. An Imbolc spring-cleaning ritual may be compared to the steps of cleansing and purifying both the self and your space before a ritual. Wiccans take the opportunity to clean earlier than their secular neighbors. We clean the house, remove Yule decorations, and spiritually purify and bless living space. Imbolc is the perfect time to do a top-to-bottom, wall-to-wall spiritual purification and subsequent house blessing. Refer back to the simple rituals you have created for personal purification, and rework them to be applied to your living space.

Imbolc is also a time to purify ourselves of any negative baggage, both spiritual and emotional, that we have carried with us through the winter. Take time to meditate on how you would like to sweep away the negativity from your life, and create a ritual to reflect this.

Above all, Imbolc is a wonderful celebration of creativity. Exercising creativity is a life-affirming way to reflect the fertility of our spirits. Creating sacred space and engaging in your favorite creative activity—whether you write, sketch, paint, sing, play an instrument, cook, bake, quilt, knit, or do anything else artistic— is a wonderful way to celebrate Imbolc.

Take the corn dolly made at Lughnassadh (see the section on Lughnassadh for instructions) or wrap a bundle of twigs in a blanket and leave them by the fireplace or your altar with a wand (or some other phallic representation) overnight to encourage fertility in various areas of your life. As Imbolc prepares the way for the return of spring and proof of life in general, such an action symbolizes your desire for that fertile energy to be reflected in your life, and also reflects your faith that spring will indeed return.

Ostara

March 20–23: when the sun passes into the sign of Aries

Ostara is a modern festival celebrated on the spring equinox. Unlike the solstices, there is little evidence that pre-Christian people celebrated the equinoxes, and thus the equinox festivals tend to be even more obscure in their sources than the other sabbats.

The name of this modern spring festival is popularly thought to be derived from that of a Saxon goddess of spring, Ostre, Ostara, or Eostre. The first recorded mention of any such goddess is in Bede's 703 c.e. work, *De temporum ratione*. Bede, a Benedictine monk, stated in Chapter Thirteen of his work that the Saxons called the fourth month *Eosturmonath* after their goddess Eostre. Bede's assumption served for centuries as the source of unquestioning conflation of season with this proposed goddess, thereby perpetuating the myth that there did indeed exist a deity by the name of Ostara. Ronald Hutton postulates in *The Stations of the Sun* that Bede's association of the word indicating the season of spring with an existing goddess was, in fact, little more than a creative leap. Other than Bede's statement, there is no evidence of the existence of such a deity in the Germanic mythos, not even in the *Edda*, the main source of Germanic myth and deities.

The Saxon word *eastre* translates roughly to "beginning," which extends the Saxon use of the term *Estormonath* to mean "month of beginnings" or "month of openings"—basically their term for spring. The English word *east* is likely derived from the same etymological root in the Germanic language group, a root associated with the concept of dawn, light, shining, and new beginnings. Most other languages use the Hebrew base *pasah* to describe the festival of rebirth, fertility, and light.

All these concepts are associated with the vernal equinox, when light and dark are balanced during the inexorable increase begun by the sun at the winter solstice. While there is little concrete evidence to support the existence of a goddess called Ostara, there are goddesses in other cultural pantheons who serve the same purpose and whose names derive from similar roots, such as Eos and Aurora.

Ostara is one of the least-celebrated holidays in the modern Wheel of the Year, and this is in all likelihood due to both the tenuous connection to an obscure deity and the overwhelmingly Christian overtones to the season. Easter is celebrated in a rather Pagan fashion with plenty of pastel colors and sweets formed into the shapes of bunnies and chicks, and the decorating and hiding of eggs—all symbols of fertility originally consumed to attract similar energies to the one who ingested them.

In a way, the spring equinox sits in an awkward position between two other springlike festivals. Imbolc celebrates the returning light, the first signs of spring, and the stirring of fertility in herd animals, whereas Beltaine takes for itself the joyous celebration of fertility between man and woman. The vernal equinox is thus left with little to define it other than the sowing of crops.

Whether the Saxons did indeed honor a goddess by the name of Ostara during the fourth month, or whether Bede mistakenly postulated a deity of that name, widespread use of this goddess-form to personify spring has, in a sense, created her for the modern practitioner who wishes to mark the spring equinox as the other three seasonal points are marked.

Celebrating Ostara

Although Ostara is technically the celebration of the first day of spring and the second fertility festival, being bracketed by Imbolc and Beltaine can limit the associations applicable to this sabbat. Perhaps one of the clearest associations possible is the planting of the first crops, and it is this association that you can honor and incorporate into your own practice.

The seed is a powerful symbol, indicative of new beginnings and the potential for life. At Ostara the return of fertility to the land that began at Imbolc is now complete and is celebrated. Themes of growth and planning for future crops (spiritual and otherwise) surround this sabbat.

In the Wiccan mythos both the God and Goddess are youths, just beginning to enter their sexual prime; they exhibit signs of fertility but are not yet prepared to consummate their union. This signifies a point of balance between child and adult. Ostara, like the autumn equinox, demonstrates another point of ultimate balance: the twenty-four-hour period is shared equally between precisely twelve hours of daylight and twelve hours of night.

Eggs and seeds tend to be the symbols used in Ostara rituals. Design your ritual to draw upon some of the abundant fertile energy of nature in spring, and direct it toward an area of your life that could do with a shot of productive, creative energy. You can do this by sprouting seeds to later plant in your garden or a window box, or by sprouting edible seeds to eat alone or in a salad to literally consume the power of spring, thereby internalizing it.

Beltaine

May 1 or April 30, or when the sun reaches 15 degrees of Taurus

Beltaine is one of the two major Wiccan festivals. Beltaine and its partner across the Wheel, Samhain, stand out as the two major holy days, focusing on life and death, respectively. There are some Wiccans who celebrate these two festivals and no others.

The related themes in Beltaine are sexual fertility and the blessing of fields and newly sprouted crops. This is one of the most secularized holy days in the Wheel of the Year. In some areas of western Europe the games and traditions associated with May Day have carried on. The neo-Pagan focus on this time of great fertility and growth has resurrected a general secular interest in these games and traditions in North America.

Beltaine is the third and final festival of fertility. For the ancient Celts, who recognized only two seasons (growth and suspension), it was the beginning of summer. The word *Beltaine* has several spellings, and is most likely connected to the root words that also sourced the name Belenos, a Celtic god of fire and sun.

Many of the traditions associated with Beltaine parallel those found at Yule, such as the raising of a treelike structure, the gathering of greenery and the weaving of it into garlands, and the exchange of gifts. Both festivals confirm life.

As of the spring equinox the God and Goddess have reached their fertile stages. Now at Beltaine they physically and spiritually join together to celebrate their union. Beltaine celebrates the theme of the Great Rite on several levels. As the ultimate celebration of life, joy, sexual union, and procreation, it echoes the merging of male and female energy to perpetuate the cycle of life and nature.

This sabbat is a celebration to honor life in all its forms, just as Samhain is the celebration to honor death as an essential part of the life cycle. And as at Samhain, it is said that the veil between the worlds is thin. This means that the otherworld, the realm of the gods, magic, and spirits, is very close to our world. At Beltaine it is less difficult to connect to the realm of the gods through ritual or meditation because of the greater harmony that exists between the energies of our world and the energies of the otherworld.

Beltaine is a time of great joy, but it is not a time simply for sexual licentiousness, as more puritanical folk through the centuries have perceived it to be. The physical sexual act is one of the methods by which we perpetuate life, but in the grander scheme sex symbolizes so much more than mere physical pleasure; it mirrors the act of creation.

Celebrating Beltaine

Beltaine can be an uncomfortable sabbat for some Wiccans, for the Great Rite is often presented as an act that must be shared by two people. With so much emphasis on sex, we sometimes forget that the symbolic act can be as powerful as the physical act.

Making the symbolic Great Rite the center of your Beltaine ritual can stir your soul deeply, particularly if you write a personal invocation to speak while you lower the athame into the cup. Drinking of the cup's contents afterward with awareness and intention can also energize you with the passionate and fertile energies of the festival.

The traditional Beltaine pastimes, such as choosing a king and queen of the May (representatives of the Goddess and God) and raising and dancing around a Maypole, are often seen as beyond the capabilities of a small gathering or a solitary Wiccan. However, just as you embody a blend of both male and female energy, you can crown yourself king or queen of the May (or both!) as you desire.

Raising a Maypole and engaging in the complicated dance may not be feasible, but dancing with ribbons to raise energy through which you may connect with the season is perfectly possible. Dance is a very sensual method of raising energy, particularly if you choose to aspect an appropriate deity while doing it.

Incorporating flowers and garlands of greenery brings nature closer to you. Try to perform your Beltaine ritual outdoors if possible. Of all the festivals, Beltaine deserves to be performed among the green of nature, surrounded by the living vibrant energies at their peak.

Midsummer

June 20–23: when the sun passes into the sign of Cancer

The summer solstice features the God in his solar aspect at the peak of his power. Modern neo-Pagans sometimes call this festival Litha, which comes from the Saxon word for light. Again, as with Ostara, this is a word that seems to have been associated with a general time of year—not with a specific holy day and certainly not with a deity. Midsummer is a time of great light; the days are long and the nights are short. The crops are abundant and everywhere there is life. The Goddess, like Mother Nature herself, is carrying young, and her developing motherhood is reflected in the abundance growing in the fields. Like the Empress of the tarot's Major Arcana, she is fertility itself.

Secular Midsummer rituals in Europe usually celebrate the sun at its height of power and glory, as well as the abundance of crops growing in the fields. This festival also holds within it the simultaneous realization that from this day on, the sun loses its height and brightness slightly each day. The cycle continues; the seed of destruction lies at the heart of every triumph.

Like many of the Beltaine traditions, the traditions associated with Midsummer became quite secularized and were performed all over western and northern Europe into the twentieth century. The central symbol associated with Midsummer is the bonfire, signifying the brightness and prevalence of the sun at its powerful peak.

Celebrating Midsummer

With fire codes and safety restrictions, it simply isn't feasible for many people to construct and light a bonfire. Fortunately, there are other acts that can serve as the central symbolic action of your Midsummer ritual. As a substitute for the bonfire, light candles of orange, red, yellow, and/or gold.

If the weather is clear, rising before dawn to greet the sun from a hill is a wonderful, quiet way to welcome Midsummer. This act is peaceful and yet remarkably moving. Bring a picnic of solar-associated foods, such as eggs, custard-based tarts, oranges, and lemonade. You can chant an invocation or prayer of praise while the sun rises in the sky before you.

Midsummer is also a traditional time to begin gathering herbs, particularly herbs such as St. John's wort, associated with the powers of the sun.

Lughnassadh

August 2, or when the sun reaches 15 degrees of Leo

Lughnassadh is a Celtic-based festival to open the harvest season, and it is the first of three harvest festivals in the Wheel of the Year. Intimately connected with the concept of corn and grain, Lughnassadh celebrates the success of the previous fertility festivals and of the life cycle as seed turns to fruit.

The sabbat is named for Lugh, a Celtic god, and some believe Lughnassadh commemorates the wake of his foster mother. There are many gatherings held at this time of year wherein trade and games of skill are featured, both of which are commonly associated with Lugh, known as the many-skilled god. Lugh is sometimes associated with the sun, which also corresponds to this time of year. The other major influence for this festival is the Anglo-Saxon celebration known as Lammas. This comes from the Anglo-Saxon *hloef-mas*, or "loaf mass," a Christian celebration of the first fruits of the field, the main offering of which is the bread made with the first gatherings of wheat and grain.

At Lughnassadh the parallel between the vegetation god and the crops is drawn. The grain is seen as a symbol of the body and vitality of the God himself. Thus, when the grain is harvested, the God too is cut down, and he gives himself as a voluntary sacrifice so that his people may eat. While the grain is gathered, some of the seeds fall on the ground and are ploughed under to incubate in the fertile earth until spring, thus promising that the God will rise again in the form of fresh green crops. In death there is life; the cycle of life turns anew. Sometimes the Goddess takes the role of wielding the knife to sacrifice her lover, and this provides a sense of fertilization occurring even in death.

Celebrating Lughnassadh

Lughnassadh is a festival somewhat like Ostara, in that two other major harvest festivals (celebrated at the autumn equinox and Samhain) often overshadow it. Lughnassadh provides an important point in the sequence of the Wheel of the Year, and it is an essential time to assess the beginnings of the season of harvest in our own lives. While food and feasting play a major role in most sabbats, I connect personally with the food theme at Lughnassadh because it arrives at the time of year when fresh vegetables begin to be inexpensive and plentiful in my area. The preparation and consumption of baked bread can constitute a ritual aspect of connecting to the energy of the season. My yearly Lughnassadh ritual consists of baking bread flavored with fresh herbs from my window-garden, and every year the combination of herbs is different depending on what herbs have flourished and successfully grown. If this appeals to you, choose a basic bread recipe and experiment.

Create a Corn Dolly

A common craft associated with Lughnassadh is the creation of a corn dolly. The corn dolly symbolizes the spirit of the grain in the fields, and can make a lovely focal point for your Lughnassadh ritual. Apart from an altar decoration, there are several ways to use the dolly in your ritual, all of which symbolize the perpetuation of fertility in some way. You may burn it and save the ashes to scatter in your garden to bless it the following spring; you may bury the entire dolly in the earth and leave it to slowly decompose over the winter, thereby enriching the soil; or you may keep it and use it in your next Imbolc ritual. If you do the latter, burn or bury it once Imbolc is over, and make a new dolly the following Lughnassadh.

What You Need:

- 6 husks from fresh cobs of corn (you may also use grass or raffia if you wish)
- String (approximately 2 feet)

What to Do:

1. Take five husks and neaten them so that they all lie on top of one another lengthwise, with the ends roughly even.
2. Bend them in half and tie a short length of string just below the fold to create a head.
3. Take the sixth husk and fold it in half, then slide it crosswise into the open end of the husks and push them up to rest against the tied-off portion to create arms.
4. Tie another piece of string just below the cross-piece to secure the arms. Tie off hands if you wish. You may leave

the body as it is for a female dolly, or divide the husks into two portions and tie off legs to create a male dolly.

Harvest

September 20–23: when the sun passes into the sign of Libra

Of the three sabbats associated with the harvest, Harvest is the major festival of thanksgiving and plenty. Held on the autumn equinox, it is also called Mabon by many modern neo-Pagans because of the Welsh myth of a hero traveling to the underworld to rescue Mabon, paralleling other harvest-related Indo-European myths of rescuing young people from the underworld.

At Harvest you celebrate successes for the achievements they are, and you also engage in reflection upon how those successes came to be. It should be remembered that Harvest is still a season of activity and work. No crop is ever gathered by sitting back and congratulating oneself upon how well it has been tended. This sabbat balances that activity with pause to give due recognition to the effort involved in every step of the process that led to current success. Harvest embraces both the hard labor and the necessary rest that punctuates labor.

Balance is an important theme associated with this sabbat—as it is with Ostara, the vernal equinox. Again the hours of day and night keep pace; again light and dark meet as equals. From this day forward, the darkness will gain upon the light, which will continue to fade in a more noticeable fashion.

The God is still recognized as occupying the role of sacrifice, giving his life so that the cycle of life and death may continue. The concept of sacrifice is not limited to loss, however. All sacrifice is made so that others may gain. In these two sides we again have balance and a sense of equality. The Goddess is seen as a provider, a matron bearing a cornucopia of bounty and health, who provides even as she mourns the loss of her lover. Like Imbolc, this festival is associated with hearth and home as well as family.

Harvest marks the threshold of light and dark, the fine line between life and death. While the solstices celebrate the point where an extreme is reached, the equinoxes focus on liminal states, the moment where a precise balance moves to one side or another of a still point.

Celebrating Harvest

Any ritual associated with Harvest usually focuses on giving thanks for the abundance in your life. This is an opportunity to give thanks for even the very small things that make your life bright and joyous. Meditate upon what makes your life unique and complete, and what makes it happy, and bring that list of blessings to your main ritual. Give thanks to the gods by offering them food, incense, flowers, or some other kind of gift. The magic of giving thanks is that it reaffirms those blessings. By recognizing the positive elements of our lives, we invite even more positive energy to flow to us. Every Harvest you can compose a new grace to be said in ritual, in which you invite the blessings of the gods to fall upon the food and drink of the year to come. In that grace you can also thank them for their many blessings. Alternatively, instead of offering a new prayer of thanksgiving every year, you may write one to be used every year; the sense of connection to previous and future Harvests may be more appealing to you.

You may also wish to reach out to your community at this time of year by donating to a charity, or by bringing food to a local food bank or clothes to a shelter. What we give out freely returns to us in like kind three-fold, according to the Wiccan Rede.

Like Yule, Harvest is a time that can be shared with your non-Wiccan family and friends. Plan and host a dinner party, as formal or informal as you wish it to be, and cook and bake if you so desire. Alternatively, organize a potluck evening and ask everyone to bring a dish of a certain category, such as appetizer, entrée, salad, bread, or dessert.

Samhain

October 31, or when the sun reaches 15 degrees of Scorpio

Samhain is the third and final harvest festival in the Wheel of the Year. As the seasonal year is a wheel, this final sabbat is also the beginning; all ends hold within them the promise of a new birth. The ancient Celts recognized only two basic seasons—summer and winter. Just as summer begins with Beltaine, so does Samhain signal the beginning of the winter season.

Samhain marks the time of quiet and reflection that will occupy our minds and hearts until Yule, or Midwinter, when the God will once again be reborn. At this time the Wiccan mythos recognizes the Goddess as the wise woman and crone, walking by our side as we reach the end of the cycle, escorting us to death and the underworld, where the God now reigns and awaits us with love. Samhain marks a period of solemn introspection and evaluation, and subsequently the preparation for the fallow period, when the earth sleeps and regenerates its energy. As at Beltaine, the veil between the worlds thins. The otherworld, or spirit realm, seems much closer to us, and we are allowed to communicate with those beyond the veil. This offers a great opportunity for divination, both to gain insight into the previous year and to offer some sort of guidance as the Wheel begins to turn again.

With its solemn focus on the importance of death as an essential element within the cycle of life, it is perhaps unsurprising that Samhain is also the celebration of ancestral dead, and the period of mourning for the slain God. Samhain is the Wiccan season of death and honoring those things and people gone from our lives but never truly lost to us. There is great emphasis placed on history and tradition in modern Paganism, and the ritual recognition of ancestors at Samhain is of great importance. The concept of ancestors is not limited to genealogical ancestry. For Wiccans, spiritual ancestors who have influenced us or served as inspiration are just as important as blood relations.

As in other sabbats, the spiritual celebration has been secularized, and the holiday of Halloween bears little resemblance to the spiritual themes associated with Samhain. Samhain is now associated with October 31, although as an intermediate Wiccan you may wish to begin calculating the sabbats by their true astronomical dates. Technically, Samhain falls on the day when the sun reaches 15 degrees of Scorpio. Since October 31 has been popularized as the date of Halloween, many Wiccans prefer to schedule their Samhain celebrations after this date to allow the opportunity to celebrate both holidays, for in truth the two are very different occasions. Many Wiccans end up celebrating Samhain during the first days of November.

Celebrating Samhain

Samhain is not a time to fool around with ouija boards or to go roaming through cemeteries looking for a spooky time. Rather, it is a festival that allows us to examine our lives and say goodbye to those projects and people who are no longer with us. In the mythological cycle surrounding the Wheel of the Year this is the time when the God descends to the underworld, having been sacrificed along with the grain of the crops. At Samhain the Goddess presents herself as the Crone aspect, the Veiled Lady who gathers the dead to her bosom, she who holds the scythe and the knife.

Samhain is a festival that our modern society has truly grasped and brought into the mainstream. Dressing up in costume echoes the folk practice of disguising children so that malicious spirits will assume that they are spirits, too, and leave them alone while the spirits carry out their mischief. The use of masks or costume in your Samhain ritual can emphasize the idea of identifying with your spiritual or genealogical ancestors, or with a deity figure associated with the sabbat. The carving of jack-o'-lanterns descends from either the practice of keeping a lantern in the window to guide the spirits of ancestors back to the bosom of their family for the night or the practice of creating glowing maleficent faces to convince the evil spirits that the house had already been targeted by one of their brethren.

As this sabbat revolves around ancestors, it is a festival that usually involves much storytelling. Lighting a candle and telling stories of your family within a ritual space has great power. Ancestors are not only blood relations; you can honor significant figures in your career path or figures from your spiritual past as well. People who have inspired you or otherwise made a positive impact on your life can also be honored in a Samhain ritual.

Some Wiccans perform a dumb supper: they lay a place at the table for those who have passed over, and serve them a portion of the meal. The meal is eaten in silence, allowing each family member to receive whatever impressions or message from the other side that the ancestors wish to communicate. This tradition is easily adapted to be a meal held within your ritual space, with a serving set upon the altar for your ancestors and another to be eaten by you and other participants in silence. Choose foods enjoyed by your ancestors, or foods you identify with them.

Esbats

The word *esbat* is thought to have been derived from the French *s'esbattre*, meaning "to frolic." As sabbats offer us the opportunity to celebrate the seasonal cycles, esbats offer the opportunity to celebrate our personal connection with the Divine through tracking the phases of the moon. In Wiccan communities esbats are an opportunity to gather and do such work as training and teaching, as well as magical work. They are an excellent opportunity to engage in exercises to strengthen your abilities and your focus, and engage in meditation and perform magical work of your own. Some Wiccans feel at a loss for what to do at an esbat. The sabbats are very clear in how they mark certain points during the seasonal cycle, but the moon phases are more mysterious and less defined. The result is that some practitioners end up casting a circle and performing a vague ritual simply because they feel obligated.

Esbats are generally associated with the Goddess. They are held according to the moon cycle, and the moon is a symbol usually associated with the feminine face of the Divine. Although popular Western lore associates the moon with feminine energy and thus with the Goddess, there is no reason why you cannot experiment in working with God energy during an esbat. If you work with a pantheon that has a male lunar deity, honoring the feminine principle at a moon-based ritual might not make much sense to you. Honor the principle that the moon represents to you. Alternatively, you could use esbats to honor both the Goddess and God.

Because esbats are associated with the moon, the unique rite of drawing down the moon is sometimes performed (see Chapter Twelve).

Wiccans often mistake esbats as solely full-moon celebrations, but in actuality esbats celebrate the moon in any phase. The full-moon association has its roots in past times, when, it is thought, the light of a bright, full moon would help revelers find their way to wherever the secret esbat was taking place in the countryside. This may or may not be true, because a full moon would have also increased the danger of being seen by unsympathetic observers. Nonetheless, the image of the full moon as the ideal time for an esbat has carried through to this day.

To use the lunar energy of the moon in any of its phases, you do not need to be working your ritual at a precise time when the moon is in the sky. Limiting yourself to working just at one moment, such as when the full moon occurs, is not only inefficient but also ludicrous. Phases don't automatically switch from one aspect to the next like a traffic light changing; they slowly blend into each other. For example, if you wish to use the energy of the waning moon, you do not need to be up at three in the morning to "catch" it. Some Wiccans worry that they must work an esbat at the precise moment of a full or dark moon. This is remarkably impractical! For magical purposes we usually consider the energy of a full or dark moon to encompass the day before and after, as well as the actual day the moon occurs in the indicated phase.

Working when you can see the moon in its appropriate phases is always special, and for particularly important esbats you may wish to schedule your ritual at a time you normally wouldn't work to take advantage of the atmosphere. If you can work near a window or outside in a safe place, try to do so simply to compare how it feels with your other esbat experiences.

The following phases may not exactly match the phases in beginner books or on wall calendars. The next sections provide a flexible system for scheduling, however, and flexibility is one of a modern eclectic Wiccan's strengths.

New Moon

The new moon, or crescent moon, always rises several hours after sunrise, although we cannot see it in daylight because of the brightness of the sun close by. The first glimpse we see of this moon is as a thin crescent, the two points facing up and to the left, low on the western horizon just as the sun has set.

When the crescent moon is first beheld, you can sometimes see the rest of the moon in shadow, nestled within that bright curve. The first signs of the new crescent arising from the body of the old dark moon provide a lovely reminder of how all things contain within them the seed of the future.

The new moon is traditionally associated with maiden goddesses, and if you choose to work with the God as well, look at son-lover figures, youthful gods, or gods associated with new beginnings. This is a time to focus your magical work on goals associated with new projects, children, and animals.

Waxing Moon

The waxing moon rises between midmorning and late afternoon, and sets around midnight. The waxing moon is a time of growth and expansion, a gathering and evolution of light and energy.

Warrior goddesses associated with defense or goddesses associated with sovereignty are aspects that resonate with the energy of the waxing moon. Though traditionally associated with active goddesses, this phase of the moon is also a good time for working with gods associated with nurture, animals, prosperity, vegetation, hunting, and building success. The Green Man is an excellent god-form to work with during the waxing moon, as is Cernunnos or any other hunter/prey god.

Full Moon

The full moon rises at sunset, achieving its full height just before midnight.

Traditionally associated with mother goddesses, this phase of the moon is also ideal for working with god-forms associated with defense, success, peace, balance, and the power of nature. Again, the Green Man is an excellent god-form to work with during a full moon.

The full moon occurs at a precise moment, just as the dark moon does at the opposite side of the phase. The energy of the full moon can begin to be felt approximately a day to a day and a half before the actual moment, and an equal amount of time after the moment as well. Experiment with your timing and keep notes. Depending on how you interact with the moon's energy, you may be able to use the full moon–influenced energy before or after the basic three days.

Waning Moon

The waning moon rises between evening and late at night. It is associated with decrease, banishing undesirable energy from your life, and limiting overactive energy or situations.

Traditionally associated with darker goddesses who rule concepts such as justice, this is also an excellent time to work with god-forms associated with protection from offensive action, such as Herne.

Dark Moon/New Moon

The dark moon, or new moon, rises with the sun, so we are unable to see it. The dark moon signals the beginning of a new lunar month, and it is the only time a solar eclipse can occur. Some Wiccans are not at ease performing an esbat when there is no moon in the sky. This discomfort is often due to learning or reading of some tradition that insists this is a time to rest and refrain from magical work. However, the dark moon is a time of equal power to the full moon, simply at the other end of the spectrum. Working with the dark moon offers you an excellent opportunity to address issues that you would prefer to leave buried deep inside. Wicca is about balance, and to deny the dark aspect of the gods their opportunity to share their wisdom with you is to skew the basic balance between light and dark that Wicca strives so hard to honor.

Blue Moon

The most common definition of a blue moon is that it is the second full moon in a calendar month. The moon is full approximately every twenty-nine days (give or take a few hours), so any month except February may see two full moons in the sky, one at the beginning and one at the end. On average a blue moon occurs only once every thirty-three months. (So "once in a blue moon" is just once in over a year and a half!) The second, lesser-known definition is that a blue moon is the third of four full moons in a single season. A blue moon is an ideal time to focus on wish magic, or long-term goals.

Celebrating Esbats

Esbats are the movable feasts of the Wiccan ritual world. They wander all over the calendar, which means that you have to keep track of the moon and what phase it is in. An esbat is similar to a free turn for the Wiccan ritualist—they're your opportunity to do whatever you like!

Esbats provide an excellent opportunity to do sabbat-associated magical work. Determine which sabbat will occur closest to the time of your chosen moon. Attempt to apply the theme of the sabbat to your esbat. For example, if your esbat is near the autumn equinox, cast a spell to bring an ongoing situation to a fruitful end or to keep your expected harvest from earlier projects moving smoothly and profitably.

There exist names for the thirteen moon cycles that reflect seasonal and cultural associations with the natural cycle as it manifests in a certain geographic area. For example, the moon in January is often called the Cold Moon, which reflects the natural climate for much of northern Europe and the northeastern American continent for that month. Take a look at the following table of moon names and see how they reflect the turning of the year according to these three cultures and locations. Remember, colonial America began as a northeastern enterprise, which is likely where the moon names for that region originated. The Cherokee moons offer a slightly different phrasing for what the climate may have been like in the Appalachian mountain area.

Month	Old English	Colonial American	American Indian (Cherokee)
January	Winter Moon	Wolf Moon	Cold Moon
February	Trapper's Moon	Storm Moon	Bony Moon
March	Fish Moon	Chaste Moon	Windy Moon
April	Planter's Moon	Seed Moon	Flower Moon
May	Milk Moon	Hare Moon	Planting Moon
June	Rose Moon	Dyan Moon	Green Corn Moon
July	Summer Moon	Mead Moon	Ripe Corn Moon
August	Dog Day's Moon	Corn Moon	Fruit Moon
September	Harvest Moon	Barley Moon	Nut Moon
October	Hunter's Moon	Blood Moon	Harvest Moon
November	Beaver Moon	Snow Moon	Trading Moon
December	Christmas Moon	Oak Moon	Snow Moon

Don't feel bound to a particular interpretation of an esbat. The moons are flexible, which means that within this Wiccan staple there is plenty of room for personal interpretation and creative freedom.

Chapter Nine

Rites of Passage

With the techniques explored in this chapter you will learn how to craft various rituals to mark or solemnize major milestones, and how to relate the events to spiritual evolution.

The Purpose of Rites of Passage

Traditionally, a rite of passage marks a time when an individual reaches a new or significant change in life. Rites of passage often serve a two-fold purpose: they can aid the individual in transition to understand a new role, and they can aid a group or society in recognizing the change. Rites of passage can alert the community to an individual's new status, informing others of how they are now expected to interact with the individual.

Most societies and cultures hold ceremonies for a handful of commonly recognized events, such as birth, entering adulthood, and death. In North American society we also celebrate certain events to commemorate smaller passages from one state to another within those major circumstances of birth, entering adulthood, and death, such as graduations, convocations, and birthdays.

A rite of passage is not simply a ritual performed to signify the end or the beginning of something. The purpose of the ritual goes much deeper than that.

Stages of a Rite of Passage

With every rite of passage there are three separate phases to be addressed:

- Separation from the old state
- Transition between states
- Incorporation into the new state

Society has devised various methods by which these phases may be defined and the transition between them made easier. Human psyche desires structure, and we seek to assign meaning to every aspect of life. The desire to create rites of passage to further define our lives and the individual stages within them is perfectly natural. Experiencing and holding rites of passage offers us the opportunity to look deep inside ourselves and evaluate who we are and what we have learned, and to prepare ourselves for what is to come. This is applicable to the individual undergoing the rite of passage, as well as the larger social group witnessing and celebrating it.

It is important to recognize that a rite of passage does not (and cannot) last for the entire duration of all three phases. Instead, it usually marks one point within that change—sometimes the beginning, sometimes the end—although it very often reflects or refers to the entire process in miniature.

Separation

In the separation phase the individual is removed from a familiar role in their environment. This separation forces the individual to adjust to a new and unfamiliar world and structure.

In its most basic sense the separation phase can be seen in the process of birth, where an infant is removed from the warm security of its mother's womb into a harsh and cold world beyond all it has ever known. Death, too, is a form of separation when the individual leaves the secure and familiar world and physical form they have come to know deeply over the course of their life.

Transition

The transitional phase offers the individual the opportunity to learn the new responsibilities and behavior expected of them in the approaching stage. The individual requires time to acquire skills and knowledge that they will need in the final state. The transitional period is a liminal state, wherein the individual does not belong to the former role and environment, nor do they yet belong to the new role and community.

The years of adolescence are a transition between the states of childhood and adulthood. Likewise, being engaged is the transitional state between being single and being married.

Incorporation

The final stage of a rite of passage occurs when the transitional phase is complete and the individual is fully incorporated into their new role within the community. The old position within the community has been completely left behind, and the individual is now fully confirmed within the new role.

Fixed Rites of Passage: Birth and Death

There are only two "fixed" points in our lives. We were born at one point, and at another point we will die. Between these two fixed points we have other liminal states or life-changing points, but these two extremes serve as key emotional moments for those involved in a community, and are deeply ingrained into our social consciousness as requiring some sort of commemoration and ritual to mark the event.

Birth Rites

Wiccaning is a common term used in connection with birth. It signifies the blessing of a Wiccan child, and the incorporation of the child into the Wiccan community or practice. In other neo-Pagan circles this rite is also referred to as a birth blessing or a naming ceremony. If you are part of a Wiccan community, such as a coven, you may participate in the introduction of children into that community. If you bear a child, then you will have the opportunity to bless your own son or daughter in the name of what you hold sacred. You may also be asked by a close friend or family member to perform a ritual such as this, if they are among the increasing number of people who no longer participate in an established religion. If you are a Wiccan who practices secretly and you have a new baby, your Wiccaning ritual does not have to be public or shared with anyone else; it can be a beautiful ritual involving just you, the infant, and nature. The gods are always present.

A Wiccaning welcomes the child to the world, and also ritually introduces that world to the infant. This rite is *not* a purification of any sort; Wiccans do not believe that a baby is born with any sin or negativity attached. Apart from the energy of the Divine, a child has quite possibly the purest energy in existence.

A Wiccaning is also a blessing of sorts. As outlined in Chapter Five, a blessing is a simple ritual by which you extend a wish to someone or something in the name of the Divine. In this instance, the child is presented officially to the gods, an act of respect before you ask for their blessing to be bestowed upon the child.

Finally, a Wiccaning can also serve as an official naming ceremony. Such a ceremony is an opportunity to confirm the child's full name in a ritual environment, or to add a magical or special God- or Goddess-name to honor both a deity and the child.

In Wicca a child represents many things, such as hope, joy, light, purity, and new beginnings. As Wiccans believe that souls reincarnate, a new baby signifies a joyful occasion when a soul has chosen to return to life upon the earth, to interact with other souls and spirits, and to learn new lessons.

A Wiccaning ritual does not have to be restricted to an infant; many parents choose to wait until their child is a toddler before they perform a ritual like this. However, a Wiccaning is definitely a child-based ceremony. See suggestions for birth-associated rituals that revolve around the parents later in this chapter.

Steps Within a Ritual of Wiccaning

Depending on how formal you want the Wiccaning to be, you may or may not wish to include the following steps:

- Creation of sacred space or casting a circle
- Invocation of elements
- Invocation of deities
- Invocation of ancestors
- Blessing and/or naming of the child
- Presentation of the child to the Divine and/or the elements
- Presentation of the child to the ancestors
- Cakes and wine shared among the gods and the participants
- Thanks and farewell to deities, ancestors, and elements
- Dissolution of the circle (if used)
- Feast

Unless you are performing the Wiccaning in an area that you consider threatening, creating sacred space will suffice. If your Wiccaning is a formal event with others present, you may prefer to cast a circle to match the formality of your ritual.

The following ritual is designed to be held outside, but it can be adapted to be performed inside quite easily.

Wiccaning Ritual

Ideally, this ritual should be performed outside, weather and season permitting. If you are performing the ritual alone, make sure the child is secured in a safe baby seat with adequate protection for the weather. If you are performing the ritual in the presence of family or friends, someone special may hold the baby when your hands are busy.

This ritual requires no specific tools, although you may use your athame or wand in the ritual opening if you usually do so. However, if you are performing this ritual in the presence of others, you may not feel comfortable using tools. Also, rules covering the use of blades in public places vary, even if the blade is a tiny one; look into your local laws before using an athame in a park, for example.

Though the baby in these steps is referred to as "they," you can use "he," "she," or whatever you like within the spoken portion of the rite.

Remember when working with an infant in ritual to be aware of their safety at all times. Exercise caution when handling objects and substances close to the child's eyes, ears, nose, and mouth. If the infant has already demonstrated sensitivities to any of the supplies listed, substitute something else of a similar nature.

Timing: perform this ritual at dawn or some point during the morning; spring is ideal for its associations with new beginnings.

What You Need:

- A small pouch (blue is a good color) to contain the talisman items
- A clean small shell
- A small blue lace agate stone
- A clean small feather

- A white candle in a candleholder (preferably a taper candle)
- A red candle in a candleholder (a votive works as well) to represent fire
- Matches or a lighter
- Fresh flower of your choice to represent air (no need for a vase; you can just place the flower on the altar)
- A small bowl of water to represent water
- A small bowl of salt to represent earth

What to Do:

1. Assemble your supplies and set up your altar in a pattern that pleases you. Place the pouch, the shell, the stone, and the feather together next to the white taper candle in the candleholder.
2. Create sacred space or cast a circle in your usual method.
3. Consecrate the elemental representations, and light the red candle.
4. Purify and bless the other supplies.
5. Call the quarters as the elements, not as watchtowers or guardians. Invite them to be present as you bless a new life.
6. Invoke the deity or deities of your choice.
7. If you are performing this ritual in the presence of others, call to the altar the adult who is carrying the child. If you are alone with the infant, bring the baby to the altar. You may leave the child in the secure seat, or you may carry them in your arms if you feel confident doing so.
8. Say: *We are present to bless this new child whose birth confirms again the miracle of life. Child, named [insert child's name here], welcome to this world. I greet you with love and with joy.*

9. Pick up the flower and touch it gently to or pass it above the child's forehead, hands, and heart, saying: *[Child's name], I bless you with the element of air. May you speak sweetly; may words and wisdom be your friends.* Place the flower back on the altar.

10. Cup your hand around the red candle for a moment, visualizing the warmth and light collecting in your palm, then lay your hand on the child's forehead or cheek, saying: *[Child's name], I bless you with the element of fire. May you always know joy, be well loved, and possess the energy to live fully and in health.*

11. Dip your index finger into the bowl of water and gently touch the baby's forehead, lips, and heart, saying: *[Child's name], I bless you with the element of water. May your sleep always be restful and your dreams sweet, and may you always adapt easily to new situations.*

12. Touch your index finger to the salt, then gently touch the baby's forehead, stomach, and feet, saying: *[Child's name], I bless you with the element of earth. May you always know stability, be well fed, and be prosperous.*

13. Stand before the altar and say: *Blessed ancestors, you who have gone before us, be here this day as we give thanks for the newest life in our family. Watch over them as they grow, and grant them your gift of wisdom. Thank you, and blessed be.*

14. If you are alone and have been carrying the baby, place them back into the seat and secure it. Light the white taper candle from the red candle, saying: *Lord and Lady, behold the new life that shines like a star. I present [child's name] to you, and ask that you bestow your blessings upon them every day of their life. [Child's name], blessed be by all aspects of the Divine.*

15. Take the small stone and move it to a clear place on the altar. Carefully tip the white candle and allow a few drops of wax to fall onto the stone. Replace the white candle carefully and pick up the small pouch. One by one, take each of the small talisman items and place them into the pouch, saying: *A stone for earth; wax from the flame of fire; a seashell for water; a feather for air. Earth, fire, water, air, sanctify this talisman created for [child's name] to guide and bless them. Lord and Lady, I ask your blessings upon this talisman. So mote it be.*

16. Show the talisman pouch to the child, and then tuck it into the child's wrappings, saying: *Earth, fire, water, and air walk with you, guide you, bless you, and protect you all of your days, [child's name]. Walk in the light and love of the Lady and the Lord. So mote it be.*

17. Take the child from the adult or from the infant seat, and face the altar. With the child, thank and dismiss the deities you have invoked, followed by the ancestors. Then move with the child around the circle counterclockwise to dismiss the quarters in reverse order. Return the child to the infant seat and secure them there, or hand them back to the adult.

18. Pour out the water onto the ground or at the base of a tree or plant as an offering of thanks. Leave the flower as an offering as well. Pinch out the flames of both candles. Wrap the white candle carefully and keep it to light on the child's birthday for a few minutes every year. Dispose of the salt in running water. Keep the talisman pouch near the child, hanging out of reach.

Alternate Birth Rituals

Although a Wiccaning is a more common ritual associated with birth, there are other rituals you might choose to perform or be asked to perform.

If you are pregnant, or if a friend is expecting, you may wish to perform a belly-blessing ritual. A belly blessing can either revolve around the mother or focus on the infant. Hopes and wishes for a safe delivery are common in both of these cases, as are wishes for protection, strength, and serenity.

In some cultural communities rituals are performed by other community members simultaneously with the actual birth process. If a family member or close friend is giving birth, you may perform a sympathetic ritual to symbolize the actual process of the separation phase for the mother and child. A ritual such as this can raise energy to charge a talisman you can later give to them, or raise energy to be available for those involved in the birthing process (should they need it).

Planting a tree in the name of the new child is a beautiful gesture. Research the trees that grow well in your climate, and then research their associated meanings and energies to select an appropriate tree. Choose your location carefully; many families plant a birth tree on their own property or the property of a family member. If you wish to donate a tree to a civic park, contact your city works or parks department for further information. Some cities will allow you to sponsor a tree in someone's name. Sometimes a plaque can be made up and affixed nearby.

A ritual to celebrate the birth of a child does not have to be done immediately. Some people may wish to celebrate this rite of passage at the next Yule, a time traditionally associated with the rebirth of the divine child, or at the next vernal equinox, a time associated with new life and youth.

Parenting Rite of Passage

When a child is born, society tends to focus on the new person who has joined the community. We often forget that the parents, too, experience a separation from their previous state, and are transitioning into a new role. They may have had nine months to prepare themselves, but no amount of reading and prenatal classes can truly prepare anyone for the reality of physically birthing a child and then bringing them home. The parents have left the state of being a couple, and now must train themselves to recognize and grow accustomed to being a family.

To that end, a rite of passage celebrating this shift can be a wonderful thing, for it provides a clear recognition of the new roles in which the parents find themselves. A ritual of this kind can be particularly meaningful for adoptive parents to perform as a formal welcoming of the child into their hearts and their home.

New Parent Ritual

You can perform this ritual for yourself, or you can perform it for a new parent or set of new parents. The child's presence is not required for this ritual, although parents may wish the child to be present, even if the child is asleep. If you are performing this ritual for yourself and the infant is present, you must secure them in a safe bassinet or infant seat.

This ritual is presented as one for a Wiccan to perform for both new parents and it is assumed there is one new child. But with very little effort you can adapt this to carry it out for a single parent or for multiple children. Perform this ritual on a full moon, at noon.

What You Need:

- A bowl of salt to represent earth
- A bowl of water to represent water
- Fresh flower(s) to represent air (one for the child, one for each parent present)
- A red candle and candleholder to represent fire (a votive is ideal)
- Matches or a lighter
- A floral crown for the mother (if present)
- A vine or leaf crown for the father (if present)
- White taper candles and candleholders (one for each new child, one for each parent)

What to Do:

1. Assemble your supplies and set them up on your altar in a pattern that pleases you.
2. Create sacred space or cast a circle in your usual method.
3. Consecrate the elemental representations and light the red candle.
4. Purify and bless the floral and vine crowns and the white candles.
5. Call the quarters as the elements, not as watchtowers or guardians. Invite them to be present as you confirm the parent(s) as mother and/or father.

6. Invoke the deity or deities of your choice, again coding your invitation as you did for the quarters.

7. Invite the ancestors of the family to be present to witness the ritual, again coding the invitation to state the purpose of the ritual.

8. Begin the rite by stating the purpose of the ritual in the following fashion: *Elements, Lord and Lady, blessed ancestors, I bid you welcome to this ritual! This day we confirm [name of mother] as a mother, a queen in her own right. For ten moons she has carried life within her, and now she has tasted of motherhood with all its joys and pains.*

   Elements, Lord and Lady, blessed ancestors, I bid you welcome to this ritual! This day we confirm [name of father] as a father, and a king in his own right. For ten moons he has watched and supported [name of mother] as she carried life within her, and now he has tasted of fatherhood with all its joys and pains.

9. Lift the floral crown in your hands, saying: *Great Mother, bless this woman as she nurtures and raises her child. Throughout this experience may she taste sweetness and joy, and may her fears be soothed; may she be strong, and understanding when times are hard; may her child grow safe and strong, knowing that he is loved and secure in the love of his mother. Great Mother, mighty Queen, we ask your blessing upon [name of mother] as she faces new experiences and challenges of motherhood, and learns more each day. Lady Goddess, by your love and light, so mote it be.* Place the crown on the mother's head, and kiss her cheek.

10. Lift the vine or leaf crown in your hands, saying: *Great Father, bless this man as he nurtures and raises his child. Throughout this experience may he taste sweetness and joy, and may his fears be soothed; may he be strong, and understanding when times are hard; may his child grow safe and strong, knowing that he is loved and secure in the love of his father. Great Father, mighty King, we ask your blessing upon [name of father] as he faces these new experiences and challenges of fatherhood, and learns more each day. Lord God, by your love and strength, so mote it be.* Place the crown on the father's head, and kiss his cheek.

11. Direct the parents to hold hands. Place your hands over theirs, saying: *Gracious Goddess, Mighty Lord, guard and guide these new parents as they take the first steps along their path. They now serve as guardians and guides to their own child, whom they love with all their hearts, as you love them. Bless their love for one another and their love for their child; bless their hearts, their souls, and their lives. Bless their family, which now includes [child's name]. So mote it be.*

12. Direct each parent to light one of the white tapers from the flame of the red candle. When the two tapers are burning, set the third unlit taper on the altar between them, saying: *Where once there were only two, now there are three. Together, you have created the miracle of life. Rejoice in this accomplishment as you symbolically join your two flames to light this third candle.* Allow the parents to touch their candle flames to the unlit wick so that the third candle lights. Direct them to place their candles on the altar on either side of the third taper.

13. Take the hand of each parent, saying: *You are confirmed as Mother, and as Father. We cherish you, for these roles are honorable, and as old as time. Congratulations. Blessed be.*
14. Thank and dismiss the deities you have invoked, then thank and dismiss the quarters in reverse order. If you have cast a formal circle, dissolve it in your usual fashion.
15. Pour out the water onto the ground outside, at the base of a tree or plant as an offering of thanks. You may leave the flowers as an offering as well, or the parents may wish to press them and keep them. Pinch out the flames of all the candles. Wrap the white candles carefully and give them to the parents; they can light them at home that night to burn all the way down in thanks, or they may choose to keep them in order to light them for a few minutes annually on the child's birthday to further celebrate the family. Some parents may prefer to do this on the date of conception (if known) or the date the pregnancy was confirmed, in order to differentiate the celebration of the family unit from the child's birthday. Dispose of the salt in running water.

Miscarriage, Stillbirth, Infant Death, and Loss

One of the more painful events associated with pregnancy is a terminated pregnancy, whether due to natural causes or medical necessity. This, too, is a separation phase, where the woman must release (however temporarily) her role as a mother-to-be, and transition back to her previous state. Many women feel the need to ritualize their fear, pain, and anger at such an event. Creating a ritual to work through this rite of passage can be very cathartic.

Such a ritual can be equally valuable for parents who lose their child in the birthing process, or who give birth to a premature infant who subsequently passes away.

Although the child is the one who dies in this case, a rite of passage to mark the event revolves more around the parents. As in the case of a crossing ritual (see the following section), this ritual addresses the needs of those left on this earth, who must cope with the trauma of the loss. Such a birth ritual is also a death ritual, which in the Wiccan view confirms the life cycle and the promise of life anew. You can create a ritual for this purpose thoughtfully and with respect by combining aspects of both rituals.

Death Rituals

Funerals and the many associated funeral customs allow us to mark the separation that occurs with death. More than a ritual for the deceased (who is not necessarily affected by the rites we perform once they have passed on), funerals help those left behind make the necessary changes to adjust to being separated from loved ones.

In Wicca a funeral is often referred to as a crossing. As Wiccans believe that existence is a never-ending cycle of lives, a funeral mourning an individual's death doesn't really suit the spiritual outlook. Instead, a crossing ritual celebrates an individual's achievements in this life, and wishes the person well on their journey to whatever next life in which they choose to incarnate.

Death is not an end in the Wiccan view; it is a confirmation of the continuing life cycle, just as birth is. In a sense, it is another form of birth, as the deceased leaves one state and transits into another. A death ritual must address the same three phases that any rite of passage addresses. As we are unsure of what precisely happens to the soul of the deceased, most death rites serve the needs of the community, easing those left behind through the separation from the deceased. For them this involves learning how to live again without the presence of the individual, and finally reintegrating with the world after grieving and acceptance.

Although death is seen as a natural part of the cycle of life, Wiccans acknowledge that it can be very hard on those left behind after an individual has passed on. In this sense, a crossing is also a farewell to the individual, and an opportunity for those who remain to share memories and grieve for their loss. It is important to remember that Wiccans do not grieve for the individual who has died; they quite naturally grieve for themselves. A crossing offers the chance to grieve with others, and to ritually address the loss.

Some Wiccans believe that the spirit of a deceased Wiccan travels to another plane of existence, where it prepares itself for the next life it chooses. This plane is sometimes referred to as the Summerland. The Summerland is also a place where a soul ultimately finishes its journey, after it has incarnated often enough to acquire as many life lessons and as much knowledge as it feels necessary. It is important to remember that the Summerland is not considered a reward, akin to the Christian concept of Heaven, nor does Wicca have a concept of a plane of punishment comparable to Hell. The rewards for how you live your life come to you while you live it.

A crossing eases the transition of the deceased's spirit from this world to the presence of the ancestors, who will care for the spirit until it is prepared to reincarnate. In a crossing the spirit of the deceased is invited to attend, much the same way the deities and ancestors are invited. Crossings can also be performed to aid a spirit who has become lost or confused in its transition. If an individual has died in a traumatic fashion, a crossing will sometimes be performed to help it detach from this plane of existence and help it on its way.

A crossing may be performed with the body or ashes of the individual present, but it is commonly performed without. Crossings are often performed as memorial services, which provide comfort and closure for those left behind. If the crossing is for a Wiccan who was a member of an established Wiccan community, the tools and religious possessions are often disposed of or distributed to those who have been chosen by the individual to next hold and use them.

Steps Within a Crossing Ritual

As in Wiccaning rituals, crossing rituals will feature common ritual elements. A crossing tends to be more solemn than a Wiccaning, and people seem to prefer a greater degree of formality in a ritual such as this. The structure is appealing to a grieving psyche, and the formality also suggests doing the deceased a greater honor. Unlike the celebration of a Wiccaning, a crossing requires a formal circle. You are invoking the presence of a newly deceased spirit, and it is essential that you protect it and provide it a place of complete security.

Does a crossing have to be serious? Of course not! If a raucous celebration of the deceased's life is more appropriate both for the community and the individual, go for it!

Apart from the necessity of casting a circle, you may or may not wish to include the following steps, depending on how formal you wish the crossing to be:

- Invocation of elements
- Invocation of deities
- Invocation of ancestors
- Opening the portal to the Summerland (usually in the west)
- A eulogy for the deceased to celebrate their accomplishments
- The farewell: a personal symbolic act to represent your release of the individual's energy
- Offerings to the deceased
- Cakes and wine shared with the deceased, the gods, and the participants
- Disposal of the body of the deceased (burial or cremation)
- Ceremonially handing the spirit of the deceased to the ancestors, and releasing it to walk its new road
- Closing of the portal to the Summerland
- Thanks and farewell to deities, ancestors, and elements
- Feast

Crossing Ritual

Performing a crossing ritual can be a very difficult thing to do, particularly if you were close to the individual who passed on. The more difficult it is, sometimes the more important it is for you to work through it, for a crossing aids the ritualist as much as the individual's spirit. Remember, a death ritual is designed mainly to allow those still living the opportunity to address their emotions surrounding the event.

What You Need:

- A white candle in a candleholder
- A cup or chalice filled with spring or bottled water
- A gift or offering for the deceased (such as a flower, food, or a handmade token)
- Matches or a lighter

What to Do:

1. Set up your altar in the western quarter of your circle. Alternatively, set it up in your usual location, but create a small secondary altar in the west. On the altar in the west set the white candle and the chalice of water. Set your gift or offering nearby.
2. Center and ground. Raise your circle.
3. Call your quarters and ask them to stand as witnesses to your ritual, coding your invocation to the purpose of the ritual.
4. Invoke the Goddess and God, coding your invocations to the purpose of the ritual.
5. Center and ground again. Stand facing the west and visualize a door or an archway forming within the west quarter. Invoke the presence of the deceased: *From the shores of the west, / I call to this circle my friend [name of deceased]. / [Name of deceased], if you are willing, join me in this temple / So that I may formally honor you and your life, / Give thanks for our friendship, / And bid you farewell. / Welcome, [name of deceased], to my circle. / So mote it be.*

208 Wicca: A Modern Practitioner's Guide

6. You may or may not feel the energy you associate with the individual, or sense that something has changed in some way. Light the white candle to signify the presence of the deceased.

7. Get comfortable, and begin to talk. Talk about the times you have shared with the deceased, the lessons you learned from the person either directly or by example, and memories in general. Allow yourself to laugh, to cry, and to communicate whatever you need to communicate. Perhaps there are unresolved issues you need to address; address them now. Perhaps you feel you need to apologize for something; do so. This is your opportunity to work out all the knotted emotion surrounding this individual's passing, to allow your grief to flow, and also to be happy for all the good things this individual accomplished in life.

8. When you are finished, take your gift or offering in your hands and hold it up before the candle. Say: *[Name of deceased], I thank you for the many blessings you have bestowed upon me during your lifetime. / If any of your energy remains with me, I return it to you with my thanks, and my love. / Go in peace; carry on in your journey. / Blessed be.* Place the gift next to the candle and close your eyes, opening yourself to release any of the personal energy the deceased may have invested in you.

9. When you feel that the release is complete, take up the chalice and say: *[Name of deceased], I drink to you / and to your accomplishments / I honor your life, and I honor your passing. / May this water wash me clean of the grief and pain I have felt, / And remind me of the joy that life brings. / So mote it be.* Drink of the water, and as you swallow visualize the

water cleansing the sadness and pain from you. Sprinkle a few drops of the water at the western gate with your fingers as an offering.

10. Replace the chalice at the western quarter, next to the candle and the gift. Center and ground.

11. Give thanks and bid farewell to the deceased: *I thank you for your presence, [name of deceased], / And for the joy you have brought me throughout your life. / May your journey continue in joy and peace. / [Name of deceased], I bid you farewell. / Blessed be.*

12. Visualize the door or archway in the western quarter fading away. Snuff out the candle to signify the departure of the deceased.

13. Thank and release the deity in your usual fashion.

14. Thank and release the quarters.

15. Dissolve your circle. Center, then ground once again.

16. You may choose to place the candle in your altar, relight it, and allow it to burn down completely; or you may keep it aside and relight it every year as an act of memorial, or include it in a formal memorial ritual on the anniversary of the death or in an original death ritual.

17. Take the gift and the remaining water outside, and either toss them into moving water or bury them in the earth in a place you associate with the person. Alternatively, if there is a grave for the deceased, you might leave them there.

While not many of us ever find ourselves in the situation where we are asked to perform a funeral for another, most of us feel the need to commemorate someone's death. Performing a private crossing ritual for a loved one, even if there's an official funeral in the style of another religion, is perfectly acceptable. It allows you the opportunity to explore your own feelings about death, as well as your relationship with the deceased.

Wiccans perform a ritual similar to a crossing every Samhain, the feast of the dead when ancestors are commemorated and we have the opportunity to say farewell to the recently deceased.

There are other forms of death rituals that a Wiccan can perform. Sometimes a loved one may be in the process of dying. In a case such as this, a ritual (performed privately or in the presence of the individual) can offer the individual peace and help them work through their own fears and concerns associated with the process of dying. As the Wiccan code of ethics directs us to care for others as we would wish to be cared for, it's recommended that you ask the individual if they would mind a rite or prayer to ease passing.

Starhawk, M. Macha Nightmare, and the Reclaiming Collective have created a remarkable and unique book called *The Pagan Book of Living and Dying* that examines death from the neo-Pagan point of view, and it is well worth a read.

If you have the opportunity to be with someone in their last hours, the creation of sacred space can help soothe tension and fear. If you cannot physically be with the individual, then perform the ritual with a formal statement after the invocations that you do this in love, and offer it freely for the individual to accept if they so desire. If the person does not accept the energy and work you do, it has not been a waste—you will have worked through important issues associated with grief and loss.

A ritual to honor your ancestors and the creation of an ancestral altar are also death-associated rituals.

Movable Rites of Passage

Between birth and death there are a myriad of points in our lives when a significant transition must be marked. In the following sections we will explore three of those points popularly recognized: the rite of passage acknowledging the achievement of adulthood; the union of two individuals in a spiritual partnership known as handfasting; and the rite known as eldering, where an individual is honored as a source of wisdom and experience. You can write your own version of these rituals using the examples, exercises, and steps outlined elsewhere in this book.

Adulthood

Like all rites of passage, an adulthood ritual marks a transition from one state to another; in this instance, it is the transition out of childhood and into adulthood. Modern society has designated the teenage years as the transitory period, as there is no one point where an individual may be forced to stop being a child and join adult society. While other cultures take the first menses of a girl or a specific age of a boy as the moment that marks the required shift between states, Western society accepts that adolescence is an ongoing evolution wherein the child learns skills and information required to function in the adult world. You may wish to conduct an adulthood ritual for your own child or children, or your friends or relatives may ask you to perform one.

A suggested alternative to a single rite of passage performed at a single moment in adolescence is a pair of rituals bracketing the teenage years. The first is performed at the beginning of the teen years to symbolize the beginning of the transitory period, and the second at the end to confirm the child's successful completion of that transition and welcome them to adulthood. In the middle you may wish to write and perform a smaller ritual to mark the first menses of a girl, or the deepening of the voice or first need to shave for a boy.

Handfasting, Handparting

While you cannot perform a legal marriage unless you are ordained as legal clergy or otherwise legally recognized by your civic laws (which vary according to the state or province of your residence), you can still perform rituals to celebrate or mark unions. A handfasting is a spiritual union, the degree of which must be clearly defined as for a set period of time, for during this lifetime, or for all lifetimes. A handparting is a dissolution of such a union.

A handfasting makes an excellent parallel to an engagement, or a trial marriage to ensure that both parties are comfortable with the arrangement. There are several examples of handfasting rituals available in books, and entire books have been written on the subject with inspiration and suggestions, such as *A Romantic Guide to Handfasting* by Anna Franklin.

Eldering

Honoring our elders is unfortunately a concept that our society is allowing to slide out of common practice. The older members of our society are living longer and remaining in the workforce beyond culturally expected retirement age. Some continue working for financial reasons or because they find their careers pleasurable.

As a result, a new classification of elders has emerged but has not yet been recognized by North American culture. The age of retirement may be approximately sixty, but our elders are active and healthy, and they now have the opportunity—thanks to both technological and medical advancement—to have additional decades in which to travel, explore, and further develop their lives, and pass along their knowledge and wisdom to the younger generations.

Whereas some people classify the transition to menopause as the point of eldering for a woman (sometimes called "croning") and default to the age of retirement for a man, the fact is that many men and women of this age are not yet prepared to recognize themselves as "elders," despite their years and breadth of experience.

Recognizing yourself as an elder can be difficult, for we rarely value our own knowledge and contribution to society. Writing a ritual to celebrate your own rite of passage into elderhood can be a challenge but also deeply meaningful. A central action, such as wrapping yourself in a new shawl or cloak, or crowning yourself with vines or a circlet to denote your new position, can be very empowering.

As with all rituals, crafting your own rites of passage for the important periods of transition within your life is an enormously rewarding experience, and one that will further your understanding of Wiccan practices and life itself.

Chapter Ten
The Power of Words in Ritual

Part of developing as a Wiccan involves refining your ability to create rituals and write various liturgical elements, such as invocations. Writing them can be a challenge. This chapter will explore the creative process and the use of prayer, invocations, chants, and meditations.

The Importance of Words

Apart from your hands, your mind, and your will, words are the most common tools that a Wiccan uses in ritual. The spoken word has great power for our psyches, and saying something aloud often gives more weight to the meaning of the statement. This is one of the reasons why so many spells direct the practitioner to say something. Speaking words written on paper or in your head brings them out of the realm of thought and into the real world.

Always remember that words are important, so choose them wisely and with respect. Don't fall into the trap of thinking that what you write must rhyme. Nothing can be further from the truth! To be sure, one of the couplets in the long form of the Wiccan Rede instructs Wiccans:

To bind the spell every time, let the spell be spake in rhyme.

However, one of the problems with rhyming is that you are forced into a very specific method of writing, and into using words that may not be your first choices. When writing a rhyming invocation, for example, people often get caught up in the rhyme instead of the intent or the emotion behind the invocation. A bad rhyming invocation has less power than a solid free verse invocation written to flow well as the ritualist says it. Furthermore, the most important thing in whatever you write is *always* the idea or the reason behind the words.

One of the arguments for writing in rhyme is that rhymes make text easier to remember. While this is true, rhyming couplets spoken aloud also tend to cause the speaker to drop into a monotone, which kills the energy you're trying to raise or keep moving. Unless every line in your invocation ends with the same rhyme sound (which is next to impossible to achieve), a rhyming couplet can be the kiss of death for whatever you're attempting.

There are factors far more important than your rhyme scheme. For example, the concepts of *rhythm* and *meter* are crucial to writing good invocations. A line that "scans" has a nice, natural rhythm and flow to it. Scansion is lacking in many invocations because many people focus on rhyme rather than on having a regular number of beats in each line of the invocation. Rhythm is important in all aspects of ritual because we inherently derive pleasure from it. Rhythm provides a pattern and creates a sense of expectation. Staying with a pattern is rewarding because we anticipate it and our expectations are met. Additionally, humans work better to a rhythm because our own heartbeat is the ultimate pattern-setter. Breaking the rhythm once it has been established can be a powerful tool, because we *don't* hear what we expect, and as a result we pay more attention.

As you progress, refining your ritual creation and execution will become more important. Intention can take you only so far. A solid invocation that flows well will ease the flow of your energy as well. In a successful invocation, for example, the subject matter, the imagery, and the technical care with which you select your words and set the rhythm will together create a pathway between the material world and the otherworld.

Invocations

When we speak an invocation in ritual, we use carefully selected words to create a change or summon a specific energy. An invocation's words alone are not magical. Although they do carry energy, simply speaking them will not accomplish what you intend. Clear visualization and focused intent must be present to channel the energy required to "move" the invocation. This active energy makes invocation unlike an act of prayer. An invocation is an expression of your will, while prayer is more of a supplication to a higher power.

Wicca employs several different types of invocations, such as elemental invocations and deity invocations, for various purposes. Throughout the ages spoken spells have also been referred to as invocations, and the spoken element of a spell is still called an invocation in some circles.

Simply dashing off an invocation and declaiming it means that you're probably not thinking about what words would best suit the situation or the object of your invocation. An invocation is the initializing force that opens a connection between you and the object of the invocation. You want your words to be as precise and as tailored as possible to achieve maximum effect and success. It's not just the form and critical execution of the writing of the invocation that make a successful invocation; it's what your invocation *sets out to do* or *does*.

The Wiccan and spiritual elements serve an important purpose in an invocation. A Wiccan invocation will usually display some or most of the following characteristics.

- *An address to a spiritual entity* connects your words and intent to a higher power. Without such an address, there is no point to the invocation. And just like a ritual with no purpose, an invocation with no purpose is a waste of energy that could be guided elsewhere to a beneficial purpose.

- *An appeal to nature* taps into the power residing in the planet and the natural world. A Wiccan derives a lot of power from the natural world. Nature is regarded as Divinity manifest, as well as the reflection of the Divine. Attuning to the cycle of the seasons and the earth cycle is key to the Wiccan practice. It simply makes sense to harness that energy into an invocation.

- *A flow of rhythm and meter* provides a solid structure for the energy you're drawing upon to build and flow smoothly. If you can say it without tripping over the words, then you've got a much better chance of keeping track of all the energy without the flow stalling or choking. If the words dance along without sounding stodgy, you're on the right track. Invocations don't have to be complicated; they need to be simple, but with enough evocative imagery and imaginative language to gather as much energy as possible. Pedestrian invocations are hard to get off the ground and are one of the most common obstacles to a smooth ritual.

- *A clear statement of your magical purpose* is essential to focus your entire psyche on the task at hand. The energy you're raising needs a goal upon which to focus as it's being raised. Without a clear image, the invocation has nothing to hang on to, nor will the process of creating the invocation be smooth—you'll struggle with it.

An invocation is basically a package of symbols that, when combined with intent and energy, are unpacked to create a connection or atmosphere in which you can work, or with which a deity can connect. A successful invocation will feature a balance of elements that blend meaning, emotion, and images, and that engage the imagination and evoke response from the five senses (for example, references to visual images, scent, touch, taste, and sound). Use strong verbs to communicate your intention.

Most important in using words and imagery in Wiccan ritual is to ask yourself how they make you *feel*. Invocations serve to create an atmosphere, to introduce or stir new energy, and to reach out to a separate energy and invite it into your space. Simply describing this action isn't going to arouse the necessary emotion to fuel the actual act. Using strong verbs and vivid imagery will stir your own emotion from the first words, and will add punch to your invocation's action.

Writing powerful invocations is much easier than you think. Practice, practice, practice! Experiment and keep detailed notes on how the invocations make you feel, as well as what kind of a result they have on the spell or ritual. One of the very best ways to learn how to write good verse is to read it. Read books of all types of poetry—blank verse, formal verse, sestinas, villanelles, sonnets, epic poetry—and read poetry from different eras and cultures. Use your ears to listen for rhythm in the sounds of nature, in music, in spoken words, in plays. Being observant can develop your awareness of rhythm, and in turn influence how you write your invocations.

Writing Your Own Invocation

A successful invocation doesn't just flow from your pen. It requires thought, work, and a bit of research. Use the following steps to work through the writing process.

What to Do:

1. Create a list of sensory elements you associate with the object of your invocation: on a blank sheet of paper write the object of your invocation in the middle, and then write every word or phrase that pops into your mind all around it. For example, if you were to write an invocation for Brigid, you might start off with a list of words like: *Ireland, milk, mantle, cattle, light, spring, lambs, creativity, poetry, inspiration, healing, wells, hearth, hearth fires, homes, childbirth, metalworking, communication.* The symbolic meanings of words, or the underlying ideas and concepts that accompany words, function most strongly and effectively in an invocation. Literal and implied meanings are less important. When we invoke Brigid, for example, we are not appealing to an actual woman who has white hands, cares for cows and sheep, and kindles fires in the home. We are appealing to the symbols that evoke Brigid in our minds, our hearts, and our spirits. Symbols are the language through which we communicate with the divine part of ourselves.

2. Do a bit of research on your object, even if you already feel familiar with it. This will offer the opportunity to discover a new piece of information that inspires you to develop your invocation in a whole new direction.

3. Copy the words from your brainstorming sheet onto an index card. At the top of the card write the object. Every time you write a new invocation, create an index card of key words associated with the object of the invocation. This will make future invocations easier. As you research, add key

words to your ongoing lists. You may discover particular phrases about your object that resonate strongly with you, such as "Brigid of the white hands" from Alexander Carmichael's *Carmina Gadelica*. Note them down on the card as well. Phrases like this can help you connect to how others see the object of your invocation.

4. Write a prose draft of the invocation using the key words that resonate most clearly for you. Don't worry about style or meter or rhyme; just write it out as a plain paragraph. This is only a rough draft for your invocation. Use everyday words, contractions, and slang; don't try to couch it in fancy language. Don't worry about spelling or punctuation for now.

5. Put away your prose paragraph and return to it after a bit of a break to review it. This forms the basis of your invocation.

6. Up to this point you have been working with words associated with your object. Now you will turn your words into an invocation, by adding the depth of emotion necessary to elicit the correct energy. Think about the images that have spontaneously formed, or that arise in your mind or heart when you read your plain prose paragraph. Play with the sequence of the words and refine them. Consider synonyms. Do not, however, deliberately construct clever-sounding imagery. Forced images will not flow properly. Often the simplest imagery becomes the soul of an invocation and the heart of the unfurling energy.

7. Formalize the language only to a point at which you are comfortable. If you are not a Shakespearean actor, don't couch your invocation in Renaissance English. Never use any word if you are not 100 percent certain of its meaning.

If a word sounds right but you still can't put your finger on precisely what it means, take the time to look it up. Don't try to write your invocation in unfamiliar language. *Thee* and *thou*, *dost* and *whence* may sound impressive when someone else says them, but in general they're grammatically incorrect. If you're not used to using such words, they can trip you up as you speak them, and this will sabotage your invocation's purpose. Trust yourself, both as a ritualist and as a writer of invocations; reflect who you are and don't try to sound like someone else.

8. Next, think about the structure of your invocation. Used with intent and awareness, devices such as rhyme scheme, meter, and form can reinforce and amplify the meaning of your invocation. Play with the form of your invocation and watch how it changes. Be certain, however, that the poetic form and structure of your invocation do not obscure the intention behind it. Don't shoehorn a gentle, flowing invocation into the stiff and structured sonnet form if it is better suited to a free-form, nonrhyming verse.

9. Read your invocation out loud. How does it sound? How does it make you feel? Does it create the effect you were looking for? If yes, then you're ready to use it in ritual. If not, work on it some more until you're happy with it.

Delivering Invocations

The repetition of a phrase or invocation can intensify the feeling or intent encoded in the words. Whether you speak your invocation only once or repeat it a chosen number of times is up to you.

The physical stance you take while you deliver an invocation has an impact on the energy you gather. Stand firmly, with your feet shoulder-width apart. Don't lock your knees; allow your body to be relaxed but alert. Center, then ground. Breathe deeply and regularly for three to five breaths. Speak your invocation with conviction. Conviction does not mean increased volume—speak with confidence, assurance, and certainty.

Daily Devotional Prayers

The difference between a prayer and an invocation lies in aim. A prayer seeks to commune with a deity or energy in some way, while an invocation seeks to invoke the presence of a deity. Edgar Cayce once outlined the difference as follows: "Prayer is supplication for direction, for understanding. Meditation is listening to the Divine within."

Prayer may be done silently or aloud, alone or in the company of others; it may be accompanied by certain body positions or actions, such as lighting a candle or incense. Prayer can be used in a variety of ways, for a variety of purposes, including:

- To further attune with the spiritual force within our lives
- To encourage certain values or beliefs in the one who prays
- To help the one who prays to focus on the deity
- To communicate with the deity

A prayer used in an honoring ritual, esbat, or rite of passage can be a beautiful addition to a ritual. Nonsupplicatory prayer is a method by which we attempt to harmonize ourselves with the greater energy of the universe and of our ultimate spirituality.

In one sense, a daily devotional is a type of mental and spiritual programming. By repeating the devotional act over and over again, you create a shortcut to the purpose of the prayer, a reminder of your connection to the Divine. It's also a shortcut to whatever state you're attempting to encourage or create—such as tranquility before bed, alertness in the morning, or release of tension and being open to the physical and spiritual nourishment of a meal. Just as celebrating the eight sabbats in the seasonal round attunes you to the overall rhythm of the year, your daily devotional prayers can help attune you to the energy of the world and your own being as those energies flow through the day. In addition, daily devotionals remind you of the cycle of the day, which in turn fits into the greater life cycles.

Devotionals provide a wonderful way to absorb wisdom regarding the relationship between humanity and the universe—a true example of the microcosm as it relates to the macrocosm, and vice versa.

Performing regular devotionals every day will help you obtain the maximum benefits of connecting to the greater energy and the cycle of the day.

A simple ritual when you get up in the morning or before you go to bed at night exemplifies the daily devotional. Saying grace at a meal also constitutes a daily devotional. Grace is a challenging devotional to do, because it often smacks of forced prayer to a monotheistic God. Saying grace, however, is perfectly within the Wiccan mindset and spiritual practice. Think of the cakes and wine rite within the larger ritual context. Although on one level the cakes and wine rite is an example of the sacred marriage and union between the Goddess and God, it is also a rite through which we thank the gods for their bounty, and their largesse in sharing it with us. This is, in essence, a very formal version of saying grace at a meal.

It would be extremely awkward, however, to perform a full cakes and wine rite before every meal. First of all, we often eat in the presence of others with whom we may not wish to share our spiritual practices. Second, Wicca does not require its adherents to formally thank the gods at every meal, as the gods are understood to be omnipresent.

Devotional Prayers Exercise

There are other ways to incorporate a spiritual devotional moment into your daily life. Take a look at the following exercise and work out what kinds of devotionals you'd like to do and when you would like to do them.

What to Do:

1. Choose three points of the day, and write a devotional for each. For balance you can choose getting up, the midpoint of your day, and preparing for bed at night. Perhaps it might be better to think about what times of the day you would like to connect with deity, or when you think you need to connect with deity. Maybe the first few minutes before you sit down to your daily job in the morning would be a good time for a quiet devotional prayer. Perhaps there is a busy point in the afternoon at which you regularly feel overwhelmed, and you would welcome a minute or two of peace.

2. Compose these three devotionals and use them daily for at least twenty-eight days, or one moon cycle.

3. Keep notes on how you feel about this exercise, and what effects you observe with each devotional.

    When the month is over, decide whether to keep all three devotionals, replace one or two of them, or add more.

Chants in Ritual Practice

Chants are a remarkably simple way to tune in to an abstract concept. As a Wiccan, you have the opportunity to create your own chants and use them as you require in ritual and spellcraft. Creating a chant is simple: you can repeat an affirmative phrase or a word directly associated with your magical intent over and over again in a singsong fashion, or you can write words to a tune you already know and sing it. This works best with nursery rhyme tunes or simple folk tunes. You absolutely do not have to be able to carry a tune or read music to use chants in your rituals. Singing words on one single note can also build up energy.

Because modern Wicca is relatively young, there aren't necessarily traditional chants passed down or associated with holy days as they are in organized religions. You can explore songs written within the past thirty years or so that have been released on albums or online. Some of these modern chants have been printed with music in songbooks, but this method of learning a chant can be a bit more challenging. To find them, type the words "pagan chant" into a search engine and browse the sites that come up. Many sites will allow you to download the songs.

One of the best examples of the use of chants in Wicca is the ever-popular Witches' Rune. There are two versions that use the same lines but arrange them according to a different rhyme scheme. One is an ABAB rhyme scheme, and the other is written in an AABB scheme.

The Witches' Rune comes to us from Doreen Valiente, who rewrote a lot of Gerald Gardner's work to make it more accessible and generally sound more pleasant to the ear. The word *rune* is of Old Norse origin and means "a secret or mystery." This is appropriate because using the Witches' Rune creates a shift in consciousness no matter how you chant it, allowing you to explore ideas in a different way. The word *rune* also suggests that there is a whole series of associations tied to the chant, which you explore as you use it more and more often. There is more to this chant than just the words and the raising of energy.

How do you use the Witches' Rune? It's remarkably easy. There's no specific tune that accompanies it, unless you want to recite it that way. Think of using a rolling tone, and deliver the rune rhythmically.

If you've ever taken any sort of drama lessons, forget what you learned and just lean on the rhythm of the words. Forget everything your English teachers ever said about reading poetry correctly too. The verse is designed to roll along, gathering a bit of volume and power as you go. You're meant to pause for a beat at the end of each line, and to stress every other syllable. This is a tool to raise energy, not a thoughtful or interesting poetic reading.

Following is an idea for how you can recite the Witches' Rune. The capitalized words are the ones to be stressed. (This is in the AABB rhyme scheme for quickness and to add punch to the delivery.)

DARKsome NIGHT and SHINing MOON,
HEARken TO the WITches' RUNE.
EAST and WEST and SOUTH and NORTH,
HEAR me AS i CALL you FORTH.

This is known as a basic iambic foot: a foot has two beats to it, with one beat stressed more than the other. The stressed and unstressed beats happen naturally; you don't have to force the rhythm while speaking or chanting it. Rhythm like this resembles a heartbeat, and the human ear appreciates this familiarity.

Traditionally, everyone present in a group chants the Witches' Rune while simultaneously moving clockwise. The combination of movement and chant raises a lot of energy, which is gathered and then directed by the ritual leader toward whatever the goal might be.

If you work alone or in a casual group, you have a lot more freedom to perform the Witches' Rune however you like. If you enjoy physical motion, try adding the movement to the words. Many people get tripped up when they try to concentrate on saying the words and dancing at the same time; try stomping or hopping in time to your words.

When working in a group, a regular well-known chant such as the Witches' Rune serves as an excellent method by which to adjust the group's mind and energy to the same level. And from that point chanting can serve to deepen the level of consciousness or raise energy for the group, depending on how the chant is performed. If you use it alone, the only person you need to balance is yourself.

There is a body of associated knowledge you can plug into by chanting the Witches' Rune on a regular basis with awareness and intention. Regular use of the Witches' Rune in this way keys your mind to the symbols and energies associated with the tools mentioned, the elements, the cardinal points, and the Divine in the form of female and male energies.

Guided Meditations

Meditation fosters self-discovery and encourages positive change through introspection. Meditation also facilitates spiritual healing through a restoration of emotional balance and the respite of peace and quiet. Regular meditation creates an increased awareness of the self and of the environment, a direct result of improving your focus and your ability to calm your inner restlessness. Victor Davich refers to this as the ability to open yourself "to each moment of life with calm awareness" (p. 31). Regular meditation also creates an improved energy flow throughout your body and environment. And finally, meditation is exercise for the mind, which strengthens your capability to visualize and handle energy in ritual.

Wiccans do guided meditations to explore our own psyche. The beauty of a guided meditation is that it provides structure but does not script the action so tightly that you are not allowed to participate. The experience you have undergoing a guided meditation will be different each time.

Meditation can be separated into two forms: active meditation and passive meditation. In *active meditation* you allow an object or abstract to evoke uncontrolled associations in your mind as you focus upon it. You can use a picture, symbol, sound, or motion to initialize your response, which may come in the form of imagined sounds, images, memories, scraps of dialogue or vision, and so forth. Wiccans commonly use a symbol, such as a tarot card from the Major Arcana, as a visual focus, and then imagine the card's image as life-sized. This allows the meditator to walk into the scene depicted on the card to explore the environment or interact with the figures there. Another popular form of active meditation is imagining a deity or mythological figure, and meditating upon that figure either by free association or by initiating a mental conversation with the figure. Active meditation is frequently used to explore problems, to brainstorm ways to move past obstacles, and to gain insight. Guided meditation is a form of active meditation.

Passive meditation is what people usually think of, for it involves a total focus on the object and implies a denial of all else. In passive meditation you do not allow your mind to wander freely. This form of meditation often involves employing a mandala or a mantra to keep the mind occupied. Passive meditation is often used to relax or disengage from the world around you, to encourage spiritual purity.

Guided meditations are essentially stories or scripts written in the present tense, starring you. They usually have such themes as encountering deity, working with animal guides, and exploring the various areas of cultural mythology. Someone usually reads the meditation aloud while the listeners relax and allow the scene described to unfold in their minds. If you are a solitary Wiccan, you will be writing and carrying out your guided meditation alone, but this in no way diminishes the experience. You can read the meditation over and over to get a general sense of the sequence of events, and then close your eyes, relax, and sink into the story, following the general plot. Or you can record the meditation by reading it aloud and leaving the appropriate silences to allow yourself a chance to interact or explore the area the meditation sets up for you.

Writing Guided Meditations

Writing your own guided meditations allows you to focus on your meditation landscape (the customary setting you see when you meditate). You can also tailor the characters you interact with in the landscape to the animals, teachers, and deities with whom you work on a regular basis.

The trick is to keep your guided meditation vague enough so that you or your listeners can create details on your/their own as you meditate, but structured enough to provide guidance. When writing your guided meditation, you must first decide on the theme.

- Is there an obstacle in your life that you wish to work through?
- Is there a situation for which you seek guidance?
- Is there a new deity you wish to meet?
- Do you wish to interact with the energies of the season to gain more personal insight into the upcoming sabbat?

Once you know the theme, decide on some key events that will occur in your guided meditation:

- Will you meet a deity face to face, or explore their culture?
- Will you meet an established guide or power animal to gain wisdom about your situation?

When you have these elements set, you can begin to draft the meditation. Start the meditation by talking the listener(s) through a basic relaxation exercise such as those found in beginner Wicca books, or the meditation exercises outlined in my book *Power Spellcraft for Life*.

Begin the action by situating yourself (or directing your listeners to situate themselves) in an established, familiar meditation landscape. If you do not yet have a default meditation landscape, take a break from writing your guided meditation to prepare one. It's good to have a regular point from which you can start any meditation. It may perhaps be a cottage, a bridge, a hill, a path, a field, or a tree. If you already have an inner temple (see Chapter Eleven), you can use that place as a starting point.

Now it's time to change the setting, but not into something dramatically different. Lead yourself along a path into a new environment and allow yourself time to explore both the route and the eventual destination. Provide yourself some clues and key pieces of information, but leave out the bulk of the creative work so that you may envision it when you are carrying out your guided meditation.

Use symbolic language, but remember that you're not trying to tell a full story. Each time you run through the same meditation, you should be able to experience something different. Use active verbs and incorporate sensory description as you write your guided meditation. This will help create an atmosphere so that you can describe what you see, what you smell and hear, and what things feel like when you touch them. Use these techniques sparingly, however. Tell yourself to look around, to breathe in and identify the smells, to hear the ambient noise.

Release pieces of the storyline bit by bit, allowing yourself plenty of time to explore between them. If you are to encounter an entity, for example, allow enough time to talk to the entity. You may give yourself spoken prompts, such as asking what kind of information this entity has for you.

When you're writing the meditation, don't assume that you know the lesson you're trying to teach. Attempting to indoctrinate yourself with a moral or a lesson in a guided meditation that you write is next to useless. The true value of guided meditations is in discovering wisdom or information you were not aware of before the experience.

When you feel you have left enough time to explore, discuss, and evolve through the guided meditation, direct yourself to thank any entities you may have met, and guide yourself back to the meditation landscape where you began your journey. Bring yourself out of the meditation firmly but gently. A solid return is a necessary part of guided meditations, like a definite ending to a story.

Your guided meditation should be written with the aim of it being between ten and twenty minutes. Any shorter and there won't be enough time to relax and get into it before it's over. Any longer and you run the risk of growing bored or falling asleep.

Once your guided meditation is written, you can record it. Make sure to leave long enough pauses between the structured sections to allow yourself the opportunity to explore and interact with the setting and action you have outlined. One of the most common mistakes is to rush through a meditation. Don't worry about leaving too big a gap; your imagination will come up with material to fill the empty space. It's better to leave too much room than to leave not enough.

If you have no means by which to record your voice, read your meditation thoroughly a few times to familiarize yourself with it and run through it completely in your mind as you remember it.

Carrying Out Your Guided Meditation

There are a few fundamental necessities to the practice of meditation. You must have a quiet environment to minimize distraction, a comfortable physical position to allow complete relaxation, and a method to relax the physical body.

It's important to relax the mind as well. A stream-of-consciousness narrative is always present in your mind. In daily life your attention is usually focused outward, and the stream-of-consciousness narrative serves to keep you alert and aware of what's happening in your environment and the situations in which you find yourself. Your own thoughts can become annoying and distracting when you settle down to meditate, however, so people often use some sort of focus to ease them into a more relaxed mental state. A repeated word (a mantra), a low humming sound, soft music, or a visual focus can all help ease the pressure of the stream of consciousness.

When to Meditate

If, like most people, you have a life crowded with family, work, and extracurricular activities, you may despair at the thought of even trying to figure out when and where you can cram meditation into your schedule. Think of meditation as an event you're looking forward to, as "me-time" rather than yet another task to schedule. Determine what you consider to be the quietest time of day. The less calming and de-stressing you have to engage in before meditation, the better. Then ask yourself when you are least likely to be disturbed for about fifteen minutes (this might not be the same as the quietest time of day for you). Finally, think about the place where you have the fewest distractions and demands placed on you. The answers to these three questions will help you figure out when and where you can schedule your meditation.

While choosing a quiet time to meditate can be beneficial, moments when you feel overwhelmed and stressed can also be good times to reset your mind, body, and emotions. Don't go for a long guided meditation at times like that; keep it simple. You may want to write or otherwise develop a standard meditation or visualization to help yourself calm down, using your familiar meditation landscape.

Regular meditation enhances the beneficial effects of the practice, and it can help you whenever you decide to engage in a guided meditation. Beginning a regular meditation practice can be a challenge to anyone. One of the most important things to remember is that you don't have to devote an hour to it every day; ten minutes a day will do you more good than an hour once a week. By booking fifteen minutes by yourself to meditate, you can take five minutes to stretch a bit and settle into a physically relaxed state. This is a good time to work on your centering and grounding techniques.

Meditation is mental exercise, so it's important to start small and work your way up. Trying to overachieve in meditation can result in frustration and can make the entire practice seem negative.

The effects of meditation are cumulative, and at first it can appear as though there's no benefit or change at all. If you can recognize nothing else, congratulate yourself simply for sitting still for ten minutes. It's crucial to cultivate patience when you meditate. This can be challenging to a modern Wiccan, who may be used to experiences that fly along and changes that occur quickly. Never apologize to yourself or anyone else for taking the time to meditate; it's essential to your spiritual development and mental and emotional health. Meditation can be an example of a daily devotional. Think of it as taking time to consciously connect with the Divine and with the spiritual energy flowing through your life.

Posture

Your physical position while meditating is as important as your mental state. Your body posture is important in any sort of exercise, and holding yourself incorrectly can actually impede the benefits you seek and even damage your body (as in any sort of exercise).

Many teachers of meditation will recommend a straight-backed chair in which to meditate, and this is a good way to begin learning the proper meditation posture:

- Keep your spine erect by imagining a string attached to the crown of your head, pulling your head up, and allow each vertebra to float in place.
- Keep your shoulders back, down, and relaxed; don't hunch them up.
- Allow your arms to rest gently on your thighs or on the armrests of your chair.
- Open up your chest by imagining that you are holding a tennis ball under each armpit.
- Don't cross your legs, and keep your feet flat on the ground. If your feet can't reach because the chair is too high, slide a book under them.

Aligning the body in this way allows the energies in your system to flow with a minimum of interference.

After the Meditation

Take five minutes after the meditation to fully return to the physical realm. Center, then ground; eat something; shake out your arms and legs or walk around a bit to get the blood flowing again and to wake up your body.

Give yourself enough time to ease in and out of your meditation as well. If you aim to meditate for ten minutes, schedule an overall block of twenty minutes to give yourself five minutes to relax before you begin, and five minutes to readjust to the world when you come out of it.

Remember that what happens between the written words is more important than hearing the words themselves. You know the words already because you wrote them. Put your energy into flowing between them and around them, and into creating what happens within the silences. When you listen to the meditation, this will also be the time to note down in your spiritual journal what happened, what thoughts you had, and what your subconscious conjured up as the missing parts of the story.

Chapter Eleven

Spiritual Archetypes

This chapter will explore the archetypes of the God and Goddess, as well as various expressions of these essences. Meditations and visualizations provide tools for you to deepen your relationship with the Wiccan deities.

The Power of Archetypes

There are several levels of entities encountered in Wicca and Western occult work. The ones most Wiccans think of immediately are, of course, the Goddess and God, whether known by the general titles of the Lady and the Lord or by specific names. There are more entities, however, and they are various manifestations of archetypal power and essence in diverse forms:

- The elements are invoked in almost every Wiccan ritual, and have associated archetypal spirits.
- Power animals and totems are often used by Wiccans in pathworking exercises.
- Ancestors are honored and invoked as repositories of knowledge and wisdom.
- Some Wiccan and Western occult traditions espouse the concept of the higher self, that part of the astral body/spiritual form that is directly connected to the Divine.

All these and more are worth exploring as you advance in your practice of Wicca, both for the knowledge they can provide and for the depth and range of experience they can add to your practice.

The God and Goddess

The word *great* suggests an ultimate source or authority, and for this reason it is often attached to the Goddess or God. The generic Western association of gods with solar energy and goddesses with lunar energy can be a limiting one. There are solar goddesses found in both Celtic and Germanic traditions. Sunna, the sun goddess of the Norse tradition, and Grian, sun goddess of the Irish, are both powerful deities in their own right. Likewise, male lunar deities exist, such as the popular Egyptian god Thoth.

Limiting yourself to one gendered energy or to one symbol can be narrow and restricting. Explore the symbols through both genders, and broaden your understanding of how male energy functions in childbirth or female energy within war.

The deities are often broken down into three or four aspects. The Goddess, for example, is said to have three main aspects: the maiden, the mother, and the crone. This concept was introduced by Robert Graves in the mid-twentieth century, although it is so appealing that people now point to ancient deities and identify them as such. Sometimes the Goddess is said to have a fourth aspect, the warrior, which comes between the maiden and the mother.

The God is also said to have three or four aspects: the son, the lover, and the wise man or the lord of death. His fourth aspect is the hunter, which, like the warrior aspect of the Goddess, comes between the son and the lover aspects. While the triple aspects are more frequently seen, the four-fold aspects actually make a lot of sense within the Wiccan mythos, as they correspond to the seasons, the cardinal directions, and the elements.

When you choose to work with a deity, or in aspecting, you can invoke into yourself either the essence of a cultural manifestation or one of these three or four aspects.

Another important fact to remember is that the Goddess and God are all three or four aspects simultaneously; they may manifest as any aspect at any time and are not bound to a sequential appearance.

Working with Dark Archetypes

One of the wonderful things about Wicca is that it does not assign a positive or negative dichotomy to the light and dark pairing like so many other religions do. Wiccans understand that light and dark are both necessary for the world to operate, and that a balance is constantly in motion. Dark defines light, just as light creates shadow to create dark.

No matter how comfortable Wiccans are with the concept of darkness, when it comes right down to working with dark deities, many shy away. They do not do so necessarily out of fear, but out of a sense of respect and self-preservation: working with dark deities is usually a rough ride. This is not to say that working with bright deities is easy; bright deities are just as likely as dark deities to take your life firmly in hand and reshape it to what it should be. It's simply that bright deities have gained a burnished appeal over time and are usually seen as gentler than dark deities.

The amount of whitewashing and projected antiseptic illusions that cloak the bright deities often misleads people into thinking that the bright deities are all sweetness and light. Most deities have a blend of dark and bright elements, and over time humanity has chosen to privilege one aspect over the other. Hecate was once a Thracian maiden goddess who cared for women in childbirth, and who carried a torch to guide those who needed direction. As she was absorbed into the Greek and Roman pantheons and their spiritual needs and outlook evolved, she became a crone goddess of terrifying curses and revenge, keeper of the ghosts and spirits of the murdered souls in the underworld. Brigid, pan-Celtic goddess of inspiration, has also been a goddess of defense and warcraft, a metalworker capable of crafting spears and swords for her people.

Dark is not the absence of light; by now you know that light does not equal good and beautiful and right, and dark does not equal evil or immoral, or even amoral. Dark means embracing the shadowed aspects of your personality and soul. This understanding should be incorporated into your practice.

Ancestors

Ancestors are an important part of Wiccan practice, but unfortunately this element is not explored as fully as others. Ancestor work tends to be relegated to Samhain, when Wiccans honor their forefathers and foremothers, both biological and spiritual.

This practice is in no way evoking spirits of the dead; it has nothing to do with necromancy. There is no forcing of anyone or anything in Wicca. The ancestors are invited—never summoned or commanded—to communicate with you. No ancestor will come to you if they do not wish to work with you.

Genealogical or biological ancestors are those of your bloodline who once had physical bodies but crossed the veil into the realm of death. One of the reasons why ancestor work is so unclear is because of the conflicting beliefs among Wiccans concerning what happens after death. If you believe that the ancestor resides in the Summerland, then accessing their energy for instruction or information is possible. However, if you believe that the spiritual essence completely reincarnates, then you run into an odd ethical dilemma. What happens if you attempt to contact and converse with an ancestor who has reincarnated?

Most Wiccans who work comfortably with ancestors believe that when they speak with an ancestor, they are communicating not with the consciousness of the individual but with their higher self. If that particular ancestor hasn't yet reincarnated, then their full energy can be accessed and communicated with.

Working with ancestors can be a fascinating and rewarding practice. You do not need to be familiar with your family tree to do it. Simply meditate and allow yourself to encounter whatever ancestor chooses to come to you first at your invitation.

If you are wary of working with ancestor energy, then look to the pantheon you work with to discover who the deity associated with the underworld or the spirits of the dead may be. In Egyptian myth this is Anubis; in Greek it is Hecate; in pan-Celtic it is shared between deities such as the Morrighan and Annwyn. Invoke this deity to be an intermediary, to convey your invitation to the other side, and to accompany an ancestor to speak with you.

Higher Self

There is a portion of the spirit or soul responsible for everyone's consciousness, termed the "higher self" in Western occult thought. This higher self is sometimes described as the part of us that is of the gods, or the part that is connected to the collective consciousness. Wiccans believe that our physical bodies are also of the gods but that the higher self is unique because it embodies divine energy and can access universal knowledge.

The higher self is what many people believe communicates with or informs us when we meditate, when we use such divination tools as the tarot, when we communicate with spirits via talking boards or spirit boards, or when we engage in automatic writing.

Before you ask a question elsewhere, take it to your higher self. You know more than you think you do. You can invoke your higher self much as you invoke a deity or a guide. Refer to Chapter Ten for ideas on writing invocations.

Shadow Self

Complementary to the higher self is the shadow self. The shadow self represents all the things about yourself that you dislike or repress—those aspects and traits that you wish to deny. The shadow self is not the evil part of you; remember, Wiccans embrace both light and dark as essential complements.

Ironically, the more you repress your shadow self, the more control it wields over you and your life. It will strive to emerge, either through explosions of anger or sly insinuation into innocent words and action. It may manifest as restless energy, leading you to pace behind the figurative bars of the cage of your life. At times the dark side of your spirit is the side you need to explore to get things done or work through an obstacle. Acceptance and understanding are essential to proper handling of your shadow self. You cannot excise it from your soul; not only is that impossible, but it's also undesirable in the extreme. Your shadow self provides necessary insight into, and support for, the bright side of your spirit.

The dark side does not wish to rule any more than the bright side of your soul wishes to reign supreme; they desire to coexist, fully accepted.

Working in Safety

One of the safest places to do archetype work is in an inner temple, sometimes referred to as an astral temple. An inner temple is a place of safety and power that you carefully and deliberately construct on your own. It does not exist on the physical plane, although it may have a physical analog or equivalent. Your inner temple is your own place of worship and ritual work, a place to begin your meditations, or a place where you may safely perform ritual that you may not be able to conduct on the material plane.

You construct your inner temple by directing energy in the astral realm through repeated focused visualization and meditation. Many people already have a vague idea of an ideal temple space that they visit when they meditate. This can be an excellent basis for a formally constructed inner temple.

Through focused ritual and repeated application of your will, the inner temple becomes a place similar to but more permanent than the circle—a place between the worlds where you are not constrained by limitations of reality. An inner temple can amplify your power, simply because it is formed of your own energy. It acts as an intensifier.

An inner temple is not a pretend place; by empowering it with your energy and applying your will, it becomes a place as real as any other that stands between the world of men and the realm of the gods. An inner temple is a reflection of the self and the higher self, a completely private world of your own. No one can appear there without your express wish. If you fail to maintain your temple through regular use and investment of energy, it will very slowly decay and fade away. A strongly built inner temple can take years to crumble.

Founding the Inner Temple

If you do not have an inner temple yet, you can construct one over a period of a few weeks. You design the floor plan for your temple; it will look however you want it to look. However, you may discover certain elements, such as a pillar, a small well or pool, or a statue, popping up in places where you didn't put anything. This is not unusual. Remember that the inner temple is a place between the worlds, and as such is in both places and neither at the same time. Input from the divine essence can also help shape your inner temple. When you discover a new element in your temple space, examine it closely and sense its energy through one of the methods introduced in Chapter Four. If the element feels benign or benevolent, leave it there—it probably has a purpose. The inner temple is a partial reflection of your psyche, and although you may not consciously put something there, your subconscious or higher self may decide that it needs whatever the object is.

Construct Your Own Inner Temple

Some occult traditions have a very formal method of constructing inner or astral temples. The method described here is informal. Keep in mind that this is only the first of several meditations wherein you will be constructing your inner temple. Do not rush through or attempt to cram as much as possible into the session. Focus on exploring what you find first, and not on

constructing an elaborate temple space in one shot. First of all, you'll wear
yourself out, and second, you won't be investing enough personal energy into
your construct to give it any permanence or stability.

What You Need:

- An incense you associate with meditation, or something light such as frankincense (do not use an incense such as myrrh or dragon's blood—their scents are too heavy and their energies may have negative effects on what you are doing)
- Matches or a lighter
- Straight-backed meditation chair (optional)

What to Do:

1. Prepare yourself as you would for ritual, by cleansing your body and clearing your mind. Prepare your physical ritual space in your usual fashion.
2. Cast a formal circle, call all four elements to witness, and invoke your customary form of the Goddess and/or God. Light your incense now.
3. When you have finished the ritual opening, take a moment to center yourself again, and then sit down. As when you meditate, a straight-backed chair is ideal. It is best not to lie down during this working meditation. Begin by taking a few slow, deep breaths to calm your body and mind.
4. Visualize yourself walking along a path. It may be a city road or a forest trail; either way, this path does not have other paths branching off from it. As you walk this path,

keep your intent of finding your inner temple clearly in your mind.

5. Eventually the path will end at a door or a gate of some kind. This door may be formally constructed and set in a wall, or it may be something as simple as a low branch or a rock set in the opening of a cave. This doorway cannot be passed through by anyone but you. Lay your hand upon the door, and it will open, for you are the key to unlock it and gain access to your inner temple. No one else will ever be able to enter this space without your invitation.

6. Step through the doorway into the space beyond. Look around you. The space may already have a rough form, as it is responding to your higher self. Take the time to explore thoroughly. If something seems vague, concentrate on it until it becomes clear. Handle those objects you can touch; breathe deeply and discern what odors the temple possesses. Listen closely to the ambient noise. All these observations allow you to interact with the temple on various levels, making it more real to you. Ask yourself the following questions to help you get acquainted with the temple space and to further connect it with your own energy.

- What are the walls made of? What color are they?
- What does the floor look like? Is there a covering of some kind?
- What does the ceiling look like?
- Where does the light come from? What sort of illumination does it cast?

- What are the representations of the four elements? Where are they?
- What is the temperature?
- What are the sounds?
- What is on the walls?

7. There will likely already be an altar somewhere in the room. Do not be concerned if it does not correspond to where you first think the altar should be. Do not be concerned if the four elements do not reflect your accustomed cardinal directions. If there is no altar, create one in the center of the space; this will be your main ritual area. Your inner temple is a place where you can set up your workspace any way you please; however, a central altar is a very adaptable setup.

8. There may be doors in this temple room. If there are, do not go through them—stay in this central room for now. It is essential to establish a strong link with your main temple room before you begin to explore or create other areas of the complex.

9. Once you know what is in the central room, take a moment or two to center again. Then leave, closing the door behind you and placing your hand upon it to lock it once again. Retrace your steps along the path until you are ready to return to your physical space.

10. Write down the impression you received while exploring your inner temple, along with as many details as you can remember. Sketch out a floor plan. Make a list of what you know to be there. Then look at your list and consider what else you wish to add.

After you've completed this first exercise, make note of your dreams for the next couple of nights. You may find that you visit your inner temple in your dreams now that you have actively recognized it. If you meditate, you may discover that you default to this temple space when you visualize yourself elsewhere. Do not be concerned about these appearances of the inner temple; they mean that your inner temple is taking root in your subconscious and you are forming an excellent link with it.

Wait for at least *three days* before repeating the ritual to return to your inner temple. Again, explore the temple space. Some of what you wished to add may have appeared in your absence. If you wish to intentionally add something, choose one object to add at a time, and be detailed and focused when you create it through this visualization. Again, handle each object you see or add; touch it, smell it, listen to it. Step back and look at it from different angles, and at how it fits into the general layout of where you found it. Does the object thematically match the rest of the room, or does it stand out in some way?

When you feel comfortable, begin to experiment with performing ritual in your inner temple space. Ritual in your inner temple is a different experience from regular ritual; it is a very focused undertaking requiring stamina and energy. If you feel tired, don't try it yet. Essentially, performing ritual in your inner temple means that you are doing the whole ritual inside your head, handling the same amount of energy you would normally handle in your physical circle. Never make the mistake of thinking that working completely in your mind or on the astral plane is "easy." It is even more challenging than physically doing ritual. The immense amount of concentration involved is staggering, and if you are unprepared or fatigued you can seriously harm yourself.

When you do ritual in your inner temple, be sure that you are well grounded and that you have access to an energy source, such as the earth or the sky. Don't make the error of using only your own energy.

At first, do your entire ritual sequence, including cleansing and purifying through your circle, your invocations, your central ritual working, and the correct ritual closing. As time goes on and you become more proficient at working in your inner temple, you may wish to permanently consecrate the space so that you will not have to create sacred space or raise a circle every time unless you wish to as part of your formal ritual structure.

Working in your inner temple can be a very rewarding experience. It certainly refines your use of energy, and it forces you to evolve your skills to match the requirements of the exercise. In a space such as this, working with any of the archetypes mentioned earlier, or engaging in any of the techniques such as aspecting or channeling, can be made safer, and can yield a deeper experience. Remember to keep detailed notes in your spiritual journal; your inner temple experiences will have much to teach you when you look back over your progress.

Chapter Twelve

Drawing Down and Aspecting Deities

This chapter looks at aspecting deities and drawing down lunar energy. Learn how to safely invoke the essence of a deity into your own body for a variety of purposes, such as divination, guidance, communion, and others.

Drawing Down the Moon

Drawing down is a very specific sort of ritual. Technically, "drawing down" refers to taking in the energy of the moon or the sun. Many people believe this to mean the assumption of Goddess or God energy at the same time. However, this is not true; an assumption like this conflates the symbol (the luminary) with the signified (the deity). When we conduct an esbat ritual, for example, we are not worshiping the moon itself—we are honoring the moon as a symbol of the Goddess in one of her aspects. When the moon's energy is drawn down for magic, the Goddess does not automatically come with it.

> The rite of drawing down the moon can be overwhelming, and takes many Wiccans years before they feel strong or confident enough to attempt it. The rite can seem basic, but each rite in practice involves a lot of control and can be extremely energy-draining. Drawing down the moon is one of the more experiential rites within Wicca. You must attempt it and actually experience it before gaining a deeper understanding of what it is and why it is done. Many Wiccans are stymied by the number of unexplained actions called for within the rite. The fact that there are two different sorts of rites generally referred to as drawing down the moon also confuses the issue.

The basic misunderstanding of the phrase "drawing down the moon" arises from some Wiccans using this technique as part of the invocation of the actual essence of the Goddess into the body of the priestess. This is a method of aspecting (discussed later in this chapter). In this situation there is often a short invocation spoken by the high priest or whoever is helping the priestess to aspect the Goddess, which helps the priestess open herself to the essence of the Goddess. When filled with that essence, the priestess will often speak. Sometimes she will deliver the standard Charge of the Goddess; other times she will speak extemporaneously. In Gardnerian Wicca aspecting in this fashion is done at every ritual to have the Goddess physically present at all times. In this kind of drawing down the moon the aspecting is performed using the drawing down of the moon's energy as a stepping-stone toward the energy of the deity.

It is essential that you know and understand which form of drawing down the moon you are going to undertake before you begin. As with all rites and rituals, you should have a clearly defined goal to visualize. Decide beforehand if you are going to fill yourself with lunar energy, or if you will aspect the Goddess in general or as a specific god-form.

Drawing Down Lunar Energy

Drawing down the moon means that you are tapping into the energy of lunar power and using it to fill yourself, fill an object, or power a spell. (This is the same process used in drawing down the sun.) The practice of drawing down the moon is remarkably straightforward:

1. Center and ground.
2. Place yourself into a receptive state by clearing your mind.

3. Establish a connection with the luminary (by line of sight or by visualization).
4. Allow the energy to flow.

Think of it as the reverse of the grounding process. You connect upward and then allow the energy to flow into you, rather than reaching down and pulling the energy of the earth up.

In drawing down the moon, you allow your mind and spirit to become suffused with the primordial energies associated with the moon, such as feminine energy, psychic energy, intuitive energy, and so forth.

Drawing down the moon does not have to be done only when the moon is full. If you perform the rite at a specific point during the phase, you are accessing the energy associated with that phase. For example, drawing down the energy of the crescent moon can help empower a ritual associated with new beginnings. Drawing down the energy of the waning or dark moon can help with defense or issues associated with justice.

Men are not excluded from drawing down the moon, nor are women excluded from drawing down the sun. A drawing has nothing to do with your gender or the gender of the luminary (luminaries are genderless, being balls of flaming gas or a chunk of rock that reflects sunlight). Needlessly limiting yourself to drawing one type of energy denies you the benefits of working with the energy of the other luminary. The following ritual deals with lunar energy, but you may use it or the alternative rituals to draw down solar energy as well. Experiment and take careful notes on your experiences and observations.

Lunar Energy Ritual

Before beginning this ritual, select the moon phase you will work with. Many people work with the full moon because it is the most universally applicable energy. Depending on why you wish to access lunar energy, you may choose the new moon or waning moon as more appropriate to your purpose. The following method of drawing down lunar energy can be used for any phase of the moon. You don't need any materials for this ritual.

What to Do:

1. Prepare yourself and your space, then cast a circle.
2. Center and ground. Breathe deeply and steadily.
3. If you are not in a position to be able to see the moon, visualize it clearly in your mind's eye as it would appear in the sky. Remember to visualize it in the correct moon phase.
4. Hold your hands up and out, as if they were cradling the moon. Allow your energy center to extend two tendrils of energy up your arms to your hands, and then up toward the moon.
5. Visualize the moon's energy pouring down in a gentle, controlled flow. Feel your energy meet that of the moon, and allow the lunar energy to flow down those energy connections into your arms and your body. Pay attention to how it makes you feel.
6. Drink in the lunar energy for as long as you desire, or until you feel "full." When you are finished, gently disengage your energy tendrils from the lunar energy, and absorb them back into your body, into your energy center. Lower your hands when you are done.

Alternate Suggestions for Drawing Down the Moon

If you are wary of taking energy into your body for whatever reason, you may prefer to draw the lunar energy into a tool instead, such as your athame or wand. Another method is to draw the lunar energy into a cup of milk or water. After you accomplish this, you may drink the liquid, absorbing the lunar energy through it instead of directly from the moon. This is a lovely way to make lunar water to keep for future rituals as well. Once the water is charged with lunar energy, bottle and label the water and store it in the refrigerator. You may wish to add a cleansed moonstone to the container to further charge the water. This is an excellent way to store the energy of the moon in a particular phase to be released at a later date when you require it in a ritual or spell.

You can fill stones, candles, and any object you desire with lunar energy with this method. Some Wiccans simply leave an object in the moonlight to charge it, but this method is more active and involves you as a participant, further keying the energy to you and your use.

What to Do:

1. Hold the tool in your hands and raise it so that the tip points toward the moon.
2. Extend your own personal energy up and out through the tool, and draw the lunar energy down as before, but do not draw it past the tool; allow the lunar energy to fill the tool to whatever degree you desire. In this method the energy remains in the tool until you discharge it toward a goal. Alternatively, you may wish to charge the tool on a regular basis with lunar energy in this manner, in which case you will not discharge it toward a goal in a spell or ritual.

Aspecting in Wiccan Practice

The practice of aspecting deities is part of what Wicca is all about. If you have already been practicing Wicca for a couple of years and have developed a particular relationship with a god or a goddess, then perhaps the time has come to try aspecting them. In regular ritual invoking a deity into yourself is usually unnecessary, although in formal ritual it can be an exciting and useful method to enhance your work. Aspecting is the deliberate invocation of a deity's energy into your body for a specified period of time. The difference between aspecting and drawing down the moon or sun is that in aspecting the Goddess or God is actually present within your body, and in drawing down the moon or sun only lunar or solar energy is present.

Usually when you choose to aspect a deity, it's because you think the deity's energy will support or assist you in completing a certain task, moving in a certain direction, or overcoming a certain obstacle. The deity's energy will complement your own energy.

Never aspect a deity you have not studied, meditated upon, and come to know deeply. Not only is it disrespectful, but it's also dangerous. While aspecting can be a wonderful way to work closely with a deity, it's hard to be prepared if you don't know what to prepare for. Aspecting should be done only once you have an established relationship with the deity, and only as long as the deity seems to be amenable to the undertaking.

If you wish to embody a particular deity for an extended period of time, particularly outside of your ritual and the defined safety of your circle, make sure that you specify a limited time period for the aspecting to occur within. Aspecting should not change your behavior radically. If it does, you should do a ritual to release the deity energy as soon as possible.

There's no rule that says a woman can only aspect a goddess, or a man can only aspect a god. At times we need a shot of the appropriate energy to achieve something in particular. Remember, too, that we all contain the energy of both the God and Goddess, and we should never feel restrained from experiencing the energy of the opposite gender.

I performed a healing ritual with four friends before an important surgery of a family member of one of the participants. After creating a strong circle, calling all four elements to be present, and asking the Lord and Lady to bless the proceedings with their presence, the man leading the ritual asked three of us to aspect specific deities in whatever fashion we desired. Each of us centered, grounded, breathed deeply, and drew the deity's energy into us as per our own preferred method. All three of us were secure in what we were doing because we had worked with our chosen deities previously, and because the three deities were from a single pantheon. While individually aspecting the deities was a powerful experience for each of us separately, the jolt of energy that passed among us when all three of us touched hands in the center of the circle was one of the most incredible experiences I've had interacting with other deity energy while aspecting.

When you aspect on your own, your self-doubt can sometimes get in the way; you can question whether it actually happened, or whether you imagined it all. In a situation where you aspect with someone else, you can reinforce the other person's experience by giving them feedback. In my experience the moment at which all three people aspecting touched hands convinced every single one of us that not only were we each aspecting, but also the deity energy we were each embodying recognized the other deity energies as well. If you are a solitary Wiccan, you will likely not have the opportunity to aspect with others, but this experience can serve to illustrate how successful the practice can be.

The Process of Aspecting

People who aspect often describe it as feeling bigger somehow, vibrating at a higher level, or having a swell of energy flowing around and through them. If you have difficulty envisioning the energy of the deities entering your body or mind, or if the idea of it just plain scares you, consider what author Willow Polson suggests in her book *The Veil's Edge*: that you try turning the practice around. Envision your own essence slowly merging with that of the deity's energy. Basically, this accomplishes a similar goal: the union of your spirit with the energy of the Divine.

Depending on what the deity requires of you during an aspecting, you may aspect to various degrees. If you are working in a group scenario, the deities involved may wish to use the priest or the priestess to deliver healing or some sort of physical message while the host is aspecting the deity. If you are working alone, you have the advantage of enjoying an immediate connection with the deity you are aspecting.

In his book *Witchcraft: A Concise Guide*, Isaac Bonewits separates the methods by which the deity manifests into four categories: divine inspiration, conversation, channeling, and possession. When the Wiccan is *inspired*, they receive abstract ideas from the deity being aspected and must interpret them alone. *Conversation* suggests that the Wiccan actually hears the deity speak, and can converse with it.

A directly *channeled* deity temporarily takes control of the voice of the Wiccan to speak aloud whether an audience is present or not. (Bonewits also terms this a *partial possession.*) When *full possession* occurs, the practitioner relinquishes complete control of their body for the deities to use as they require. During an aspecting such as this the practitioner will often not remember what occurred during the experience. Only in the case of a full possession does the Wiccan ever give up awareness or control of themselves. You make that choice as to whether you will surrender full possession.

If you are concerned about losing awareness of your actions while you aspect, have a recording device running nearby so that you will have a clear record of the message that the deity has for you. Engage in automatic writing, sketching, or drawing while you aspect so that the physical proof will be there for you when you return to awareness. A recording can be one of the easiest ways to prove to yourself that you have successfully aspected, because when you aspect an entity who speaks through you, your tone and speech pattern may change slightly, and you may use unfamiliar words. A recording will offer you the opportunity to go back and listen to what went on, and it allows you to keep a concrete record of what happened.

Aspecting is an experience that every Wiccan should engage in at least once, if not a handful of times, to explore this avenue of communion with deities. Do it after studying and meditating upon the deity you wish to aspect, and then do it within a fully crafted circle, either within your ritual space or in your astral temple (see Chapter Eleven). You can alert a close, trusted friend to what you are doing beforehand, or ask for their company during the practice. If you are not publicly Wiccan, you don't have to tell your friend exactly what you are doing. You can simply let your friend know you've been doing some heavy meditation and you'd appreciate any feedback regarding your behavior for a week or so afterward.

> If you have a deep-seated fear about aspecting that stems from control issues or from a misapprehension about what possession actually is, don't ignore that fear and charge onward simply because aspecting is a part of Wiccan practice. Address these obstacles through introspection, meditation, and ritual work. Self-confidence is crucial for undertaking the practice of aspecting deities.

It is essential that you train for aspecting in much the same way you train yourself in meditation. To exercise the skills associated with aspecting, you should become adept in meditation, be physically healthy, and be very comfortable with your ritual pattern or sequence. Construct your invocation carefully. Think through what you're saying and what you are asking of the deity in this invocation; otherwise, things may not go the way you plan for them to go.

Aspecting isn't done with frequency in Wiccan practice; it tends to be reserved for special occasions, or instances when you really need the direct touch of a deity in your life. It isn't an essential element of every sabbat or esbat ritual, for example. If you are working with a sacred dramatic retelling of a sabbat story, though, you may well aspect that deity while you act out the part.

Some Wiccans prefer to interpret being a priest or priestess in a ritual as embodying the God or Goddess. They may include an invocation specifically worded to invoke the essence of the deity into themselves after the ritual opening. For example, this is a common traditional invocation of the Goddess into the body of the presiding priestess, found in both Gardnerian Wicca and Alexandrian Wicca:

> *I invoke and call upon thee, Mighty Mother of us all, bringer of all fruitfulness; by seed and root, by bud and stem, by leaf and flower and fruit, by life and love do I invoke thee to descend upon the body of this thy servant and priestess.*

An approach such as this assumes that the deity requires or should have a physical form in which to manifest during the ritual. This can be useful in group ritual, because it allows a number of people to see and interact with the deity on a material level. If you are practicing alone, you don't require this kind of interaction, for you possess a direct link to deity as the sole presiding priest or priestess.

It is essential to be in the right headspace for aspecting. Like meditation, aspecting is difficult to achieve if your mind is overactive or you are physically tense. Mentally preparing for aspecting gets you into the correct mindset for hosting and communicating with deity.

That correct mindset for aspecting is often referred to as an *altered state of consciousness*, or a trance. An altered state of consciousness is defined as a change in how the consciousness functions, takes in information, and processes that information. Being in a trance or an altered state of consciousness does not mean that you have no control over what is happening, or that you have no awareness of it. It simply means that you're functioning on a different level.

Aspecting Example

Some traditions have complex and formal techniques surrounding aspecting, whereas solitary Wiccans have the advantage of working out their own methods. Within this section you will find a general example that can serve as an outline. It is important to be confident that the deity wishes to share its energy with you. Do not attempt to aspect a deity who has been resistant to the idea throughout your preparation and meditation work.

What to Do:

1. Cast a circle. It is imperative that you work within a formal circle when you begin your work with aspecting. Working in a circle will keep outside distraction to a minimum, and the barrier also serves to contain any wonky energy that may result from your efforts.

2. Center and ground as usual. Allow yourself a few moments to settle into a relaxed but aware state.

3. Do an invocation and/or honoring act to attune to the essence of the deity.

4. Visualize the form of the deity standing in front of you and facing you.

5. Slowly visualize it merging with you until you both occupy the same space. Continue to breathe deeply and steadily.

6. Carry on with your ritual as required.

Releasing an Aspected Deity

Something a lot of practitioners who attempt aspecting don't realize is that the deity must be released. This is for your own safety and benefit. Theoretically, you could host the deity energy until it gradually fades, but having that much foreign energy in your system can be very unbalancing, and can have odd effects on your own personality and psyche. Incorrectly handling an aspecting can damage you. To avoid long-lasting damage, always remember to officially and ritually release the deity from your body. Do this by enacting the aspecting sequence in reverse.

What to Do:

1. Center and ground.
2. Visualize the deity stepping forward, out of your body.
3. Once the deity has departed, make sure you center and ground, and do a quick energy scan down your personal energy field to ensure that no foreign energy remains. If you find foreign energy still clinging to you, remove it by smudging or purifying in some other fashion.
4. Center and ground once again.
5. Make sure to speak a thanks and farewell, as you would after invoking the presence of any deity.

It is imperative that you keep detailed records of your aspecting experiences in order to enable future aspecting practice to be as successful as possible.

Chapter Thirteen

Growing As a Wiccan

How do you measure your growth as a Wiccan? How do you keep your practice fresh? Here are some methods by which you can structure and appreciate your own evolution and spiritual growth, and thoughts on how this spiritual practice relates to the world at large.

Living Wiccan

People *choose* to practice Wicca for many reasons, including to offer recognition of the divine feminine, to show one's respect for nature, to have the opportunity for self-improvement and self-empowerment, and to show appreciation of the decentralized aspects of the religion.

How do we define the *goal* of Wicca? A common answer is "to serve the gods." We work *with* the gods, not *for* them. And while this is one of the goals of Wicca, it is not the only purpose. You can serve gods in any other religion. What makes Wicca unique?

Scott Cunningham titled one of his books *Living Wicca*, and this wonderful phrase encapsulates what Wicca truly is: Wicca is more than a practice—it's a way of life. To live Wicca means living in awareness, in peace, in balance, and in harmony. It means living with the goal of every action contributing positively, and every situation teaching you something. It means being mindful, sincere, and true. Living Wicca means recognizing the Divine in everything that surrounds you, and always being able to feel your connection to the gods and the universe.

The true goal of Wicca is to create a way of life that brings you to this state. That state isn't an end; it is a means by which you can improve your life and maintain the harmony so essential to a better life and a better world.

Incorporating Wicca Into Your Life

Wicca isn't meant to be a "sometimes" spirituality; it's meant to be part of your everyday life. Giving yourself smaller daily rituals to engage in—no matter how short and simple they are—keeps you in touch with the gods and your spirituality on a more regular basis than just esbats or sabbats. If you touch the Divine on a daily basis, it's much easier to touch the Divine on the big occasions. The human mind can be remarkably apathetic when it comes to actually stirring ourselves to do something requiring energy and input. Doing a sabbat every six weeks can be a really huge undertaking if you haven't trained yourself with baby steps in between.

Wicca should never be something you take time out of your regular life to practice. The point of a spiritual path such as Wicca is to incorporate your spiritual practice into your daily life without fuss or drama. Your spirituality should inform your thoughts, opinions, and action in daily life as well as in ritual. Practicing Wicca every moment of the day should make your life more harmonious, not more complicated.

It can be very easy to *think* about Wicca, and to slowly cease your actual ritual practice. While thinking about and reflecting upon your spiritual evolution are essential to further development, maintaining your regular daily practice is paramount. Your ritual practice is your interface with the world beyond.

Online Communities

There are a staggering number of chat rooms, email discussion lists, and bulletin boards devoted to Wicca out there. Research them as best you can before you subscribe to one, however. An appalling majority of chat rooms are a waste of time and miss the central thrust of Wicca. All too often people are attracted to

Wicca for the spellcasting and magical work, and they never move beyond that. Lists and boards like this are devoted overwhelmingly to spellwork, and while they can be fun, they offer little spiritual support. Look for something with a bit more depth.

Remember that joining a discussion list or spending time in an online community doesn't mean that you have to agree with everyone all the time. Questioning *why* and *how* in Wicca deepens and develops your understanding of your practice.

Also keep in mind that talking online to others is not the clearest method of communication. It can be difficult to bare your soul, and misunderstandings can arise. You don't have to share details about your non-Wiccan life. Occasionally you may be asked by an online friend to participate in a ritual by doing a ritual at the same time, all for a common purpose. This can be a fascinating way of participating with others. It serves to connect you to something bigger, while still allowing you the privacy of your own practice and preferred manner of ritual.

Wicca for Life

To make the most of your spiritual path, you must incorporate it into your daily life in practice and in belief. Let your spiritual ethics inform your secular ethics. Wicca is a full-time religion pervading your every action, thought, and choice. The holy days and moments of worship serve as a foundation upon which your own personal practice grows and develops. You must nourish that practice—feed it and care for it.

Living your path is the ultimate expression of your spirituality. Living Wicca doesn't mean having to wear a pentacle in plain sight, or ask for sabbat days off as religious holidays; though those are both things you may choose to do, they are not dealbreakers. It means being aware of the spiritual in the material world that surrounds you, recognizing the Divine in the everyday, and encouraging the return of harmony to our modern world, so wildly out of balance.

Some people dismiss Wicca as a path of love and light, with no guts to it. These people do not understand how powerful a path Wicca can be when nourished with willpower, attention, reflection, and energy. Wicca is power: personal power, willpower, and spiritual power. Every Wiccan, whether solitary or in a coven, develops this power by the same method: through hard work, attention, observation, perseverance, and experimentation. If you are on that intermediate plateau, I hope this book has helped you understand the hows and whys of the basics you have been performing, and given you a new insight into your practice. Honoring the themes and intrinsic Wiccan elements while being willing and free to attempt new techniques is the hallmark of a healthy Wiccan practice. As a Wiccan, you have the opportunity to exercise that joy and freedom as you determine your own personal path.

Blessed be, reader. May the gods grant you their grace. May your practice of Wicca be a joy, a comfort, and a strength to you.

Bibliography

Abrams, M.H. *A Glossary of Literary Terms.* Fifth edition. New York: Holt, Rinehart and Winston Inc., 1988.

American Heritage Dictionary of the English Language. Fourth edition. Boston: Houghton Mifflin Harcourt, 2000.

Aristotle. *Aristotle's Poetics.* Translated by S.H. Butcher. New York: Hill and Wang, 1961.

Aveni, Anthony. *The Book of the Year: A Brief History of Our Seasonal Holidays.* Oxford: Oxford University Press, 2003.

Bertrin, Georges, and Arthur F.J. Remy. "Miracle Plays and Mysteries." *The Catholic Encyclopedia, Volume 10.* New York: Robert Appleton Company, 1911. Online edition copyright © 2003 by K. Knight. www.newadvent.org/cathen/10348a.htm. Accessed January 14, 2005.

Bonewits, Isaac. *Rites of Worship: A Neopagan Approach.* Earth Religions Press, 2003.

———. *Witchcraft: A Concise Guide.* Third edition. Earth Religions Press, 2001.

Buckland, Raymond. *Wicca for One: The Path of Solitary Witchcraft.* New York: Citadel Press, 2004.

Carmichael, Alexander. *Carmina Gadelica: Hymns and Incantations.* Great Barrington, MA: Lindisfarne Books, 1992.

Cat, Grey. *Deepening Witchcraft: Advancing Skills and Knowledge.* Toronto: ECW Press, 2002.

Cooley, Keith. "Keith's Moon Page: Facts, Phases, Photos, & Folklore." http://home.hiwaay.net/~krcool/Astro/moon. Accessed February 7, 2005.

Coughlin, John. "The Wiccan Rede: A Historical Journey—Part 2: The Early Years." http://waningmoon.com/jcoughlin/writing/rede.shtml. Accessed January 18, 2005.

Crowley, Aleister. *Liber AL vel Legis (The Book of the Law).* York Beach, ME: Weiser, 1976.

Crowley, Vivianne. *Wicca: The Old Religion in the New Millennium.* Revised edition. London: Thorsons, 1996.

———. *Phoenix from the Flame: Living as a Pagan in the 21st Century.* London: Thorsons, 1995.

———. *Way of Wicca.* Originally published as *Principles of Wicca* (1997). London: Thorsons, 2001.

Cunningham, Scott. *Cunningham's Encyclopedia of Crystal, Gem and Metal Magic.* First edition. St. Paul, MN: Llewellyn Publications, 1988.

———. *Living Wicca: A Further Guide for the Solitary Practitioner.* St. Paul, MN: Llewellyn Publications, 1993.

Davich, Victor. *The Best Guide to Meditation*. Los Angeles: Renaissance Books, 1998.

Denning, Melita, and Osborne Phillips. *Practical Guide to Creative Visualization: Manifest Your Desires*. Third edition. St. Paul, MN: Llewellyn Publications, 2001.

———. *Practical Guide to Psychic Self-Defense and Well-Being*. Second edition. St. Paul, MN: Llewellyn Publications, 1998.

Doreen Valiente Foundation. "The Charge of the Goddess." www .doreenvaliente.com/Doreen-Valiente-Doreen_ValientePoetry-11 .php#sthash.CTOCJzJi.0KJUE3ba.dpbs. Accessed March 5, 2019.

Edgar Cayce's Association for Research and Enlightenment. "Edgar Cayce's Meditation for Everyone." www.edgarcayce.org/ the-readings/meditation-for-everyone. Accessed January 21, 2005.

Farrar, Janet, and Gavin Bone. *Progressive Witchcraft: Spirituality, Mysteries, and Training in Modern Wicca*. Franklin Lakes, NJ: New Page Books, 2004.

Farrar, Janet, and Stewart Farrar. *A Witches' Bible: The Complete Witches' Handbook*. Custer, WA: Phoenix Publishing, 1996.

———. *The Witches' Goddess: The Feminine Principle of Divinity*. Blaine, WA: Phoenix Publishing, 1987.

———. *The Witches' God: Lord of the Dance*. Blaine, WA: Phoenix Publishing, 1989.

Fitch, Ed. *Magical Rites from the Crystal Well*. St. Paul, MN: Llewellyn Publications, 1984.

Franklin, Anna. *A Romantic Guide to Handfasting: Rituals, Recipes, and Lore*. St. Paul, MN: Llewellyn Publications, 2005.

Gantz, Jeffrey, trans. *The Mabinogion*. London: Penguin Books, 1976.

Gardner, Gerald B. *The Meaning of Witchcraft*. Lake Toxaway, NC: Mercury Publishing, 1999.

George, Demetra. *Mysteries of the Dark Moon: The Healing Power of the Dark Goddess*. New York: HarperCollins, 1992.

Harrow, Judy, et al. *Devoted to You: Honoring Deity in Wiccan Practice*. New York: Citadel Press, 2003.

Hutton, Ronald. *The Pagan Religions of the Ancient British Isles: Their Nature and Legacy*. Oxford: Blackwell Publishers, 1993.

———. *The Stations of the Sun*. Oxford: Oxford University Press, 1997.

———. *The Triumph of the Moon: A History of Modern Pagan Witchcraft*. Oxford: Oxford University Press, 1999.

Kelly, Aidan A. *Crafting the Art of Magic, Book 1: A History of Modern Witchcraft, 1939–1964.* St. Paul, MN: Llewellyn Publications, 1991.

Lipp, Deborah. *The Elements of Ritual: Air, Fire, Water and Earth in the Wiccan Circle.* St. Paul, MN: Llewellyn Publications, 2003.

Mathers, S. Liddell MacGregor, trans. *The Key of Solomon the King (Clavicula Salomonis).* York Beach, ME: Weiser, 2000.

———. *The Book of the Sacred Magic of Abramelin the Mage.* New York: Dover, 1976.

Melody. *Love Is in the Earth: A Kaleidoscope of Crystals.* Updated edition. Wheat Ridge, CO: Earth-Love Publishing, 1995.

Morrison, Dorothy. *Yule: A Celebration of Light and Warmth.* St. Paul, MN: Llewellyn Publications, 2000.

Nock, Judy Ann. *A Witch's Grimoire.* Avon, MA: Provenance Press, 2005.

Online Etymology Dictionary. www.etymonline.com. Accessed April 8, 2019.

Pierson, Dilys Dana. "Forsaking Wicca?" *SageWoman*, No. 48, Winter 1999–2000, p. 12–15.

Polson, Willow. *The Veil's Edge: Exploring the Boundaries of Magic.* New York: Citadel Press, 2003.

Rauls, Venecia. *Second Circle: Tools for the Advancing Pagan.* New York: Citadel Press, 2004.

RavenWolf, Silver. *Solitary Witch: The Ultimate Book of Shadows for the New Generation Solitary Witch.* St. Paul, MN: Llewellyn Publications, 2003.

———. *To Light a Sacred Flame: Practical Witchcraft for the Millennium.* St. Paul, MN: Llewellyn Publications, 1999.

Reclaiming Collective. *Chants: Ritual Music from Reclaiming & Friends.* Sebastopol, CA: Serpentine Music Productions, 1997.

———. *Second Chants: More Ritual Music from Reclaiming & Friends.* Sebastopol, CA: Serpentine Music Productions, 1997.

Reed, Ellen Cannon. *The Heart of Wicca: Wise Words from a Crone on the Path.* York Beach, ME: Weiser, 2000.

Robinson, B.A. "Shared Belief in 'The Golden Rule': Ethics of Reciprocity." Ontario Consultants on Religious Tolerance. www.religioustolerance.org/reciproc.htm. Accessed January 18, 2005.

Sheba, Lady (Jessie Bell). *The Grimoire of Lady Sheba.* St. Paul, MN: Llewellyn Publications, 2001.

Starhawk, M. Macha Nightmare, and the Reclaiming Collective. *The Pagan Book of Living and Dying*. New York: HarperCollins, 1997.

Telesco, Patricia. *Advanced Wicca: Exploring Deeper Levels of Spiritual Skills and Masterful Magick*. New York: Citadel Press, 2000.

Tuitéan, Paul, and Estelle Daniels. *Essential Wicca*. Freedom, CA: Crossing Press, 2001.

Valiente, Doreen. *Witchcraft for Tomorrow*. Custer, WA: Phoenix Publishing, 1987.

Wikipedia.com. "Prayer." http://en.wikipedia.org/wiki/Prayer. Accessed January 21, 2005.

Wilborn, Bruce K. *Witches' Craft: A Multidenominational Wicca Bible*. Fort Lee, NJ: Barricade Books, 2005.

Index